Urban Trees

A Guide for Selection, Maintenance, and Master Planning

Leonard E. Phillips, Jr., ASLA

McGraw-Hill, Inc.

New York   San Francisco   Washington, D.C.   Auckland   Bogotá
Caracas   Lisbon   London   Madrid   Mexico City   Milan
Montreal   New Delhi   San Juan   Singapore
Sydney   Tokyo   Toronto

Library of Congress Cataloging-in-Publication Data

Phillips, Leonard E.
    Urban tree: a guide for selection, maintenance, and master
planning/Leonard E. Phillips, Jr.
       p.   cm.
    Includes index.
    ISBN 0-07-049835-0
    1. Trees in cities. I. Title.
SB436.P45   1993
635.9´77´091732—dc20   92-43723
                                                 CIP

1 2 3 4 5 6 7 8 9 0 DOH/DOH 9 9 8 7 6 5 4 3

The sponsoring editor for this book was Joel Stein, the editing supervisor was Stephen M. Smith, the designer was Susan Maksuta, and the production supervisor was Suzanne W. Babeuf. It was set in Palatino on a Macintosh system.

Printed and bound by R. R. Donnelley & Sons Company.

*To Carol,
Kristine, Suzanne, and Michelle*

Contents

Preface

Although this book is titled *Urban Trees: A Guide for Selection, Maintenance, and Master Planning*, it could also have been called *Municipal Street Tree Master Planning* because it is intended to describe a typical street tree master plan. If the reader wants to prepare a municipal street tree master plan, this book will serve as a guide.

Moreover, if an individual is interested in the most up-to-date information on specific subjects, this book is useful for that purpose as well. For example, the latest in tree planting techniques in an urban setting can be found at the end of Chap. 4, tips for pruning street trees can be found in Chap. 5, and a clear, concise definition of integrated pest management can be found right after "Root Problems" in Chap. 5.

Regardless of how this book is used by the reader, it should be considered a guide to urban forestry in the 1990s.

Another important purpose of this book is to educate the general public regarding the proper care of municipal street trees. Since President George Bush wants people in the United States to plant 1 billion trees per year throughout the 1990s, without proper care most of these trees will fail to reach maturity.

Tree planters must learn (1) what trees to plant that will survive in urban conditions; (2) where trees should be planted so that planters will know which trees grow healthy and to maturity without impeding human activities; (3) to care for trees in their first few years at a new site to ensure survival; (4) to prune trees early in their life so they will grow straight and tall and typical of their species; (5) to care for trees so their pest and disease resistance functions to the maximum extent; and (6) to celebrate trees and their benefits to people, the environment, and the world.

Leonard E. Phillips, Jr., ASLA

Acknowledgments

I would like to extend my gratitude to my assistant, Ron Despres, arborist for the town of Wellesley, Massachusetts. I spent many hours with Ron, evaluating and discussing various portions of this book, during the past 13 years. Ron also helped with proofreading and editing to ensure accuracy and a comprehensive review of all the subjects covered in this book. I am also very appreciative of Irene Kent, who spent so many hours composing, typing, revising, and worrying over this book at the word processor.

To both of you, a special thanks.

Also, I offer thanks to those who provided technical assistance during the development of specific chapters. These individuals are noted at the end of each chapter.

Massachusetts champion—American hornbeam.

1

Introduction to Urban Trees

The planting of street trees has become very scientific and highly specialized. Because so many things must be taken into consideration when trees are planted along our streets, it is most important to select the right trees and place them properly for permanent growth and lasting beauty.

To select the right trees, an inventory must be taken of the existing street tree population. Once you know what you have, you can begin to see what is necessary to maintain the existing forest as well as where future trees can be planted, what varieties should be selected, and what is required to ensure a long life for beneficial trees. The inventory can also be used to project maintenance needs and the overall health of the existing urban forest.

Maintenance needs, the forestry department, local codes and regulations, and the importance of celebrating trees are all discussed in detail in this book.

Value of the Municipal Arborist

Many community leaders ask whether an arborist and an urban forestry program are necessary in their community. The answer is that someone should be available to organize and supervise a tree planting program to enhance the city's urban environment. Once the trees are growing, proper maintenance is necessary to ensure the health of trees and that trees do not become a liability to the city. This is where the municipal arborist can provide continuous and professional help to manage the urban forest.

Whether a professional employee is necessary or a contractor can be hired to provide this service is subject to much speculation. For example, landscaping contractors can plant trees and be supervised by contracted landscape architectural firms. Follow-up can be handled by an arborist and tree care contractors. Unfortunately, contractors will do only the job for which they were hired. Quality control, responses to residential complaints, and emergencies usually require full-time city employees. Yet full-time employees require year-round salaries, benefits, expensive equipment, and money for expenses.

Pesticide spraying is a whole story by itself, and the concerns of environmentalists are restricting the pesticide options of the municipal arborist. Most spraying has ceased except for what contractors do under municipal supervision, and even the contractors are having some difficulty in obtaining the necessary liability insurance.

The answer to this dilemma lies in obtaining high-quality, full-time personnel who will operate the program in the most professional manner possible. The professional personnel must search for ways to do the job more efficiently. If employees are informed and well trained, they can provide knowledgeable responses to inquiries from the public and will be able to handle any assignment efficiently. The arborist should also join a professional organization and be active in that organization by attending meetings and working on committees. By staying involved, people become more informed.

A local volunteer support organization, park commission, or tree board can also encourage the development of programs tailored to the needs and desires of the community. The tree board and professional staff can work together to offer positive programs such as Tree City—USA and Arbor Day as well as seedling distribution programs to school children and a department open house in the springtime. All these programs encourage public support of municipal tree management and the tree department.

Value of Urban Trees

Why should all this planning be undertaken for the sake of a few trees? Because people love trees and most communities are proud of their trees. Trees can be used by people to provide a sun, sound, and wind screen; to improve the quality of living; to provide privacy; to screen out unsightly views or to enhance good views; and to add beauty to our environment through a tree's graceful shape, colorful foliage, fragrant flower, and unique fruit.

Trees have a monetary value from enhancing real estate in addition to the value of the wood. Trees can give a community its character and identity. Trees can attract tourists to a beautiful community. Trees also provide cooler, cleaner air. They provide food and shelter for wildlife.

Tree in autumn.

Additional Benefits of Urban Trees

Trees

- Improve personal health
- Create feelings of relaxation and well-being
- Provide privacy and a sense of solitude and security
- Reduce air pollution
- Conserve water and reduce soil erosion
- Save energy
- Modify the local environment
- Reduce noise pollution
- Reduce glare and reflections
- Provide shelter from wind
- Are natural air cleaners, removing carbon dioxide from the air and releasing oxygen
- Slow rainfall runoff in the urban environment
- Make life more enjoyable

Furthermore, trees provide valuable contributions to people and the

Aerial lift crew from Lakewood, Ohio. (*Photo courtesy Donald G. Yates.*)

environment. For example, 78 trees are needed to absorb the carbon dioxide and produce the oxygen for one person; 20 trees are required to offset the pollution of a car driving 60 miles per day; trees provide a natural summer air conditioner, shade, wind control, and food and shelter for wildlife.

Trees also have some negative aspects. For example, tree roots lift sidewalks and block pipes; branches block street and merchant signs; branches and trees fall down in storms, block our streets, and eliminate our electricity; leaves are an expensive cleanup problem in the fall; and trees usually conflict with utilities for space. The resolution of these conflicts is the major reason for a street tree management plan.

The management of the urban forest first requires a review of the resources, inventory, and identification of the trees and their condition in a community. Once it is known what exists, the next question is, What is needed? What are the goals and objectives of the city, its forestry department, the managers, the tree management program, and the planting program? All this information is combined into the street tree master plan. This plan evaluates the inventory, the city, and the forestry department and then provides a planting list. Other details follow about each aspect of the total urban forestry program.

An Historical Introduction to Municipal Arboriculture

The planting of trees was first recorded 4000 years ago on Egyptian tombs and later in the Assyrian parks in 700 B.C. The Hanging Gardens of Babylon in 600 B.C. provided vegetation within an urban setting. Greek cities in 500 B.C. contained plane trees and poplars. These trees were irrigated with runoff carried in stone channels. Spanish, Islamic, and Muslim gardens used figs and plane trees to cool and shade their homes.

Urban forestry as we know it today probably began in the 1200s when rows of elms were planted in England adjacent to their cathedrals. Later, in the 1600s, trees were being planted in Paris along its network of tree-lined boulevards and avenues. During the early 1700s in England, major efforts were undertaken to plant trees for ornamental reasons in urban parks and along London's streets to improve the city's environment.

In colonial times in the United States, village greens in the center of town provided a meeting place, a place for animals, and some aesthetic relief. The use of trees in the urban landscape copied the techniques used in Europe. In 1635, Boston ordered all the trees removed from the neck connecting the city to the mainland. The

Black squirrel at Arbor Lodge, Nebraska City, Nebraska.

wood was used for building lumber and wood fuel, while eliminating the forest cover which provided ambush for robbers. In 1646, however, Bostonians realized that the loss of forest caused floods and erosion and offered no shelter from intense summer heat. The first public shade tree planting in the New World occurred that spring when a large number of men planted American Elms. The children carried water to the trees while women prepared the food.

In the 1800s more cities began to plant and protect city trees. The planting of tree species from Europe was quite popular until the mid-1800s. Native species gained popularity in the 1850s along with fruit trees that were popular in the nursery trade. Beginning in the 1860s, China and Japan opened their doors to the world, and a flood of new species were introduced that became excellent urban trees.

During the 1850s, landscape architecture in the United States was born along with the use of native instead of introduced species. Some of the leaders in this movement were Andrew Jackson Downing, Calvert Vaux, and Frederick Law Olmsted. Soon after the Lewis and Clark expeditions, new material from the west coast led to the introduction of evergreens to the landscape.

The rise of horticulture as a science also occurred in the 1800s. The Massachusetts and Pennsylvania horticultural societies are

Gypsy moth—
female and pupae.

generally credited with having a major influence on the selection and planting of trees in the urban environment. The planting of elms on Boston Common in the 1810s was followed by Lynn, Massachusetts, when that city first planted street trees, according to modern principals, in the 1830s. The city of Worcester, Massachusetts, opened its first city park in 1870.

In 1872, J. Sterling Morton, a farmer and legislator, then living in a relatively treeless Nebraska, proposed that an annual Arbor Day be observed especially for the purpose of planting trees, a practice that is now observed in most of North America. The holiday grew out of a local campaign conducted in Morton's newspaper to plant trees on Nebraska's treeless prairie. He bought 160 acres of barren land and immediately began planting a grove. Today his home, transformed into a park known as Arbor Lodge, contains 150 different varieties of trees and shrubs. His son Joy in 1922 founded the 1500-acre Morton Arboretum in Lisle, Illinois, with about 4800 different types of plants. This arboretum is among the largest of its kind.

Note that one of the early texts of the twentieth century dealing with street tree maintenance and arboriculture practice was issued by a forester of great renown, B. E. Fernow, in 1911. This was the beginning of forestry education and arboriculture in Canada. Fernow preferred that the term *tree warden* be applied to the care of street and lawn trees. Towns in Massachusetts and other northeastern states had tree wardens appointed as early as the 1700s. Professor Solotaroff in New Jersey also published the book *Shade Trees in Cities and Towns* (John Wiley, 1911), which is considered one of the first and best texts on the subject of urban shade trees.

In 1869, gypsy moths were accidentally released in the United States, and problems began about 20 years later. The devastation brought about by gypsy moths was probably the most important factor that led to the creation of laws dealing with arboriculture and the need to educate and hire municipal arborists.

From 1893 to 1916, Dr. George E. Stone served as professor of botany at the University of Massachusetts. His scientific discoveries evolved into modern-day tree surgery. He was deeply concerned with the urbanization of the United States and the impact that the expansion of utilities aboveground and below was having on our street trees. Stone also served from 1900 to 1915 as tree warden of Amherst, Massachusetts, and spent many years dealing with legislation to license arborists and the valuation of shade trees.

In 1899, the office of tree warden was established in every city and town in Massachusetts. Three years later, the first professional forestry organization, the Massachusetts Forestry Association, was

Top and bottom right: Two photographs of Arbor Lodge, Nebraska. The one at the bottom shows the extensive planting around the house. *Bottom left:* Portrait of J. Sterling Morton (*courtesy National Arbor Day Foundation*).

formed to provide training and technical assistance to the tree experts. Although this organization was first dominated by foresters, urban foresters later became predominate; today the utility arborists dominate the organization.

With so many new insects and plant diseases, new pesticides were being developed that required expertise to use. New trees and shrub varieties were also being introduced. A short course for tree workers was established in 1913 at the Massachusetts Agricultural College. At the close of this first short course, through the efforts of Stone, 25 classmates formed the Massachusetts Tree Wardens and Foresters Association. The first annual meeting was held in August 1913, when Stone was elected president. Colleges in Michigan in the 1920s and Ohio in the 1930s began to offer forestry programs, and in 1947 the first degree in arboriculture was issued. One of Stone's pupils, John Davey, wrote an excellent book which separated forestry from arboriculture. He also founded the Davey Tree Company, one of the leading tree maintenance firms in the United States.

With the advance of Dutch Elm disease, phloem necrosis, and oak wilt came a recognition of the need of knowledge to cope with them. Research was directed to many universities, and the need for experience in shade tree management was recognized by many cities. The individuals who requested the research and had to cope with the diseases became the city forester, the tree warden, or the municipal arborist in a park and tree department, park and landscape division, shade tree or forestry department. University courses to study urban forestry as an integrated urban forest ecosystem were first introduced at the University of Toronto in 1965.

The loss of urban elms to Dutch Elm disease (DED), beginning in the 1940s, increased public awareness of the bleak environment that resulted from the loss of trees. This encouraged an interest in tree planting programs everywhere. In 1936, the Shade Tree Laboratory at the Massachusetts Agricultural College was established as another response to the threat from DED. This was soon followed by the Waltham, Massachusetts, Field Laboratory which became a focal point to save and promote municipal arboriculture. Although in the first half of the twentieth century most cities began urban forestry programs, it wasn't until the 1960s and 1970s that urban forestry became a separate profession. Foresters began communicating with environmentalists, and the specialty of environmental forestry developed in leading communities. This was coupled with the trend of the 1950s and 1960s to move into the suburbs where there was a higher value placed upon the trees and homes with trees around them.

Federal Regulations

In 1967, a citizens' committee recommended to the President that the U.S. Forest Service develop an urban forestry program to provide technical assistance to the cities. The 1971 Urban Forestry Act was passed to offer urban forestry programs while continuing to provide technical assistance. The 1978 Cooperative Forestry Assistance Act expanded the commitment to urban forestry with technical and financial assistance.

Under this program, funds were given to the states for administration and distribution to any community requiring technical assistance to develop forestry programs. As a result of this financial catalyst, many communities, private tree companies, and individuals responsible for tree maintenance took advantage of these grants to develop urban tree programs.

Two components of these urban tree care programs were the complete inventory and the comprehensive street tree master plan. The inventory consisted of a counting and analysis of the existing street trees within the community. Consideration was also given to computerization of the inventory to facilitate data retrieval and keep the records up to date. The development of a comprehensive street tree master plan was to document and summarize the inventory and to provide the analysis needed to permit the development of a comprehensive street tree master plan for tree planting and management.

This program lost momentum in the 1980s and it wasn't until the end of the decade that global warming and the greenhouse effect aroused public concern. This concern led to the desire for solutions, and this in turn led to the election of our "environmental President." President George Bush developed a program called America the Beautiful (ATB) as part of the 1990 Farm Bill. ATB funding is for urban and community forestry programs, including a state urban forestry coordinator, development of a state urban forestry plan, and assistance in the operation of a state urban forestry council. Additional funding goes to rural forestry programs and for the development of a private nonprofit foundation called the National Tree Trust. This trust will promote public awareness of the importance of trees and provide financial assistance to grass-roots volunteers for the planting of trees. It is also anticipated that the foundation will begin to raise dollars to help "reforest" U.S. communities.

The ATB initiative also calls for the planting, maintenance, and improvement of 1 billion trees per year over the next several years. Of this total, 30 million trees per year would be planted in urban communities across the nation.

The Small Business Administration has also been awarded funds to provide assistance to small businesses that will plant trees on land owned by the state or local government. These businesses must be available to provide rapid increases in employment opportunities for up to 100 employees.

Definitions

The following list of definitions is an attempt to sort out the differences between commonly used phrases in urban forestry:

Urban forestry deals with the management of all wooded vegetation within urban areas.

Municipal forestry deals with the establishment, protection, and maintenance of all wooded vegetation on public land within urban and suburban areas.

Arboriculture deals with the cultivation of trees and woody plants. This is the most general term used to describe this subject.

Municipal arboriculture deals with the establishment, protection, planting, and management of trees and shrubs on public land within urban and suburban areas. This is the most specific term dealing with this subject.

Urban Forestry Associations

There are a wide variety of associations that deal with urban forestry. The primary one is the Society of Municipal Arborists (SMA). The SMA was founded in 1964; it is a society devoted to research and education subjects in municipal arboriculture. The founders had sought better representation and more time at the International Shade Tree Conference's (ISTC) annual meeting. When they were not successful, they decided to split away and form a new society.

The International Society of Arboriculture (ISA) deals with the entire spectrum of arboriculture, and it contains several special-interest groups. These include the Municipal Arborists and Urban Foresters Society (MAUFS) and the Utility Arborists Association. The ISA began in 1924. A separation by The National Arborist Association (NAA) caused fracturing of the ISA in 1938. Although the NAA remained a wing of ISA for about 20 years after separating, the NAA began holding its own conventions, and today it is a completely separate organization.

In 1969, the MAUFS was formed to meet the needs of municipal arborists. A major association battle for members occurred in the

Citizens Caring for Trees Since 1875

TREE CITY USA

early 1970s as the SMA and MAUFS struggled for growth. In 1982, a memorandum of mutual understanding was signed between the SMA and the MAUFS. This agreement allowed for the presidents of these two organizations to meet and discuss items of mutual concern and, with approval of their respective executive boards, to release joint statements of facts and concerns. The concept behind this agreement was to provide better communication and a stronger voice for urban forestry without having a merger.

The American Forestry Association (now called American Forests) has been publishing information about urban forestry since 1910 and developed the National Urban Forest Council (NUFC) in 1981 to promote an appreciation of the benefits of the urban forest. The NUFC has become a powerful organization and has been attempting to become the leading organization for urban forestry, with full-time personnel running the organization and an abundant funding source. Although this organization has promoted urban forestry, it has caused a splintering effect to the existing urban forestry organizations. This is especially a problem when NUFC biennial meetings are held because many urban foresters with limited funds attend these meetings instead of their other society meetings. One of their major campaigns has been to promote tree planting through a program called Global ReLeaf.

The Society of American Foresters (SAF) created an Urban Forestry Working Group in 1972. This group developed a comprehensive definition for urban forestry and continues to provide some support for urban forestry programs.

The National Arbor Day Foundation (NADF) was founded in 1972, one hundred years after the first Arbor Day celebration. This group, now numbering 1 million members, serves an educational function by passing technical information to its members. The NADF also sponsors the very popular Tree City—USA program and is beginning the Arbor Day Institute which will provide training programs for lay and professional municipal arborists.

History of Street Tree Master Plans

The first indication of the need for information pertaining to urban tree management went back to the 1920s. It wasn't until the 1970s, however, that a nationwide interest in street tree inventories developed. This coincided with a desire to organize pruning efforts citywide instead of on demand, which was recognized as being inefficient. In the late 1970s, inventories gained popularity as approximately one-third of large U.S. cities had or considered making one. The late 1970s and the 1980s also saw a trend of using arboricultural consultants to prepare the inventory, analyze the data, and prepare a master plan.

The street tree master plan was largely unknown until the late 1970s when a few U.S. consulting firms and municipal arborists experimented with writing them. It is remarkable that all these independent actions achieved similar results in both the approach and the format of a plan. Local deviations were the only significant difference. They all contained an evaluation of the inventory, an evaluation of the community, local regulations, and a planting plan. Later plans became more elaborate and comprehensive.

During the 1980s, as computerization became affordable and widespread, the need for accurate, up-to-date inventories and carefully designed street tree master plans became apparent in cities everywhere. The consulting firms and universities which designed these programs were able to customize each plan for the specific needs of the community.

Notable Municipal Arborists

The list given below highlights notable forestry professors and is based upon information the author has received: Dr. George Stone, mentioned above, was the first botany professor to teach arboriculture in his classes. Another spokesperson for urban forestry in the United States was Professor John W. Andresen, formerly forestry chairman at Southern Illinois University, Carbondale, and then director, Urban Forestry Studies Programme, at the University of Toronto and now at the University of Illinois. L. C. Chadwick of Ohio State was also very active in ISA as its secretary/treasurer and later executive director from 1936 to 1969. Other prominent professors of urban forestry include the following: Gene W. Grey, professor and assistant state and extension forester at Kansas State University, was formerly a service forester for the Missouri Department of Conservation. He is also very active in the Society of American Foresters. Frederick J. Deneke is with the Department of Agriculture's Forest Service. Prior to this, he was an assistant professor of horticulture and forestry at Kansas State University. Other notable professors include Dr. Robert W. Miller of Stevens Point, Wisconsin; Dr. Richard Harris of Davis, California; Dr. Alex Shigo of Durham, New Hampshire; Don Welch and Nina Bassuk from Cornell; Curtis May at the USDA; Spencer Davis from North Brunswick, New Jersey; Frank Santamour at the National Arboretum; Ray Hirt of Syracuse; Forest Strong, Karl Dressel, Carl Fenner, and J. James Kiebaso from Michigan State; and Gordon King, professor at the University of Massachusetts from 1950 to 1983.

Some of the most well-known and nationally recognized municipal arborists include Arthur A. English, tree warden of Boston; Victor J. Jarm, superintendent of parks of Hartford, Connecticut; Darrell C. Middlewood, superintendent of forestry of Birmingham, Michigan; James T. Oates, city arborist of Richmond, Virginia; Edward J. Schrader, commissioner of forestry of St. Louis, Missouri; Don Warren of Brookline, Massachusetts; Noel Wysong from Cook County, Illinois; Robert C. McConnell of Philadelphia; and Richard Abbott of ACRT.

Some of the most outstanding municipal arborists include the following men:

Edward H. Scanlon, 1903–1976

Edward Scanlon. (*Photo courtesy Society of Municipal Arborists Proceedings.*)

In 1932, Ed Scanlon was appointed city arborist in Santa Monica, California, and founded the Western Shade Tree Conference in 1934. The organization became the western chapter of ISA, and Scanlon served as executive secretary for its first 8 years. In 1936, the Committee for a National Arbor Day was organized by Scanlon, and he served as national chairman until his death 40 years later. Scanlon began his magazine in 1937, which became *Trees*. In 1946, Scanlon was selected as commissioner of shade trees for Cleveland, Ohio. During the next 9 years he planted 85,000 trees as he experimented with new trees and new ideas, especially the concept of "fitting a tree to the space available." By 1950, he had selected the Cleveland Norway Maple, the Almira Maple, the Armstrong Red Maple, Tilford Maple, and the Gerling Maple for their unique form and use under utility wires. Seeing a commercial need for these trees, Scanlon left Cleveland and began Scanlon's Nursery. Scanlon later developed eight other selections including the Scanlon Maple, Rancho Cherry, Chanticleer Pear, Flame Ash, Doric Maple, Cavalier Maple, Rancho Linden, and Scanlon Pink Bird Cherry. Known as the "wandering arborist," he became an international authority on street trees, as he lectured all over the world.

Jacob J. Gerling, 1896–1979

Jacob J. Gerling. (*Photo courtesy Society of Municipal Arborists Proceedings.*)

Jake Gerling became assistant superintendent of parks and maintenance supervisor of the Durand-Eastman Park in Rochester. Gerling was a leader in the practice of using the right tree in the right place. He also had a famous slide collection that numbered 5000. The slides were used in the numerous lectures he gave. He also wrote many articles for nursery and gardening publications. In recognition of his arboricultural ability and talents, the Gerling Red Maple, with its broad pyramidal form, was named after him.

Frank Karpick. (*Photo courtesy Society of Municipal Arborists Proceedings.*)

Frank E. Karpick, 1902–1990

Frank Karpick became a forester for the city of Buffalo, New York, in 1930 and retired as city forester in 1968. His professionalism was recognized by other arborists, who elected him the first president of the SMA, a fellow in the SMA in 1967, and an honorary life member in 1978. His other honors include being made a director of the ISA. He was also honored by George Schichtel, who named a beautifully shaped maple in his honor. In many ways he has become known as the father of municipal arboriculture for his efforts to initiate unique tree plantings along city streets. He used trees with variegated foliage, crabapples, hawthorns, hackberries, hornbeams, and other nontraditional street trees. He surveyed each city street to evaluate soil and site conditions for trees and worked to slow the spread of Dutch Elm disease. He was also instrumental in perfecting the concept of block planting of street trees.

John G. Firsching

John Firsching spent 30 years of service in the forestry department of Wichita, Kansas. During his career he was credited for park and street tree diversity in the city. He used 100 different species and developed the philosophy that "We must work along with nature and not allow any single type to become predominant."

Robert Skiera

Robert Skiera has taken advantage of his position as Milwaukee city forester to encourage urban forestry programs, both locally and nationally. Milwaukee's high-budget forestry program is considered a model of efficiency, thoroughness, and effectiveness. Skiera developed the concept of considering trees as a vital component of a city's infrastructure—"a street without trees is an abbreviated s——t." Skiera's technique was to plant trees in every city councilor's district, in order to protect the entire planting budget.

Urban Forestry of the Future

What will the twenty-first century bring? This question causes considerable speculation from experts everywhere. This is especially significant in the future of urban forestry, which should see a considerable amount of change. Biotechnology will continue making rapid advancements in genetic engineering, forestry, tissue culture, nursery stock, engineering, biology, etc. Weather forecasting should become much more accurate. Crops and trees will be developed that resist disease and insects. Cold resistance may be created through genetic manipulation, so you might see palm trees growing in the northern plains. More trees will be bred with straight trunks; or have high fiber content for the pulp industry; or be square so there is little waste at the sawmill; or be resistant to pests; or have better flowers and colored leaves; or be tolerant of poor soil conditions; or grow rapidly and still be storm-resistant; or be drought-tolerant; and combinations of all the above.

Forestry departments, however, will not be prosperous. As the U.S. population continues to age and fewer young workers are available or desire tree work to replace our retiring work crews, wages will have to see dramatic increases to be competitive as well as to entice and keep qualified personnel. These facts make forestry departments very susceptible to taxpayer cutbacks.

Energy conservation techniques and productivity improvements, which reduce municipal costs, will probably be offset by inflationary increases in nursery stock and other materials. Computers will continue expanding our horizons of use and convenience. Fiber optics and fax machines will expand our communication skills. All the new technologies will be intended to make our jobs and our lives easier and more efficient.

The current trend of planting trees to improve our environment should continue. This is no longer a fad. The President's national tree planting initiative to plant 5 to 10 billion trees in the 1990s will help. Hopefully, when all this is over, emphasis will be placed on maintaining our investment in trees. If you are active and participate, you *can* make a difference.

Sources

ACRT: *Hanford, California, Street Tree Plan*, Kent, OH, 1990.
Basile, Fred C. (ed.): Massachusetts Tree Wardens and Foresters Association, "The Golden Year Edition," Haverhill, MA, 1962.
Campana, R. J.: Unpublished notes, "A History of Arboriculture in North America," University of Maine, Orono, 1991.
Gaasland, Dale: "Congress Passes 'America the Beautiful,'" *City Trees*, March/April 1991, p. 3.

Grey, Gene W., and Frederick J. Deneke: *Urban Forestry*, Wiley, New York, 1978.
Phillips, Leonard E.: "Twenty-Five Year History of the S.M.A.," SMA, Wellesley, MA, 1989.
Phillips, Leonard E.: "The Demise of Urban Foresters," *City Trees*, May 1986, p. 14.

Endnote

Special thanks for technical assistance to Dr. H. R. Dennis Ryan III (University of Massachusetts) and Dr. Richard J. Campana (University of Maine, Orono).

2
Municipal Street Tree Master Plan

Objectives and Summary

The municipal street tree master plan is much more than a list of streets with tree assignments. The street tree master plan is a comprehensive review that evaluates the city, its trees, its forestry department, and its citizens. The purpose of having a street tree management program is to ensure that a community will continue to appreciate the benefits of trees through proper arboricultural management of the urban forest in a cost-effective manner. It is the goal of the *municipal street tree master plan* to state what is necessary for the management of the urban forest and to describe the measures and services required to fulfill these responsibilities to the community. The plan is summarized in detail in Table 2.1. Each item is defined as follows:

1. *Inventory.* The inventory is the counting and description of all municipal trees growing within a community. The development of a street tree inventory is described in more detail in Chap. 3.

2. *Analysis.* Once the inventory is completed, it can be analyzed in the master plan. The analysis might include such items as the observation of needs, problems, and value and the comparisons between items such as the relationship between species and vigor or vigor and location. It can also be used to look at diversification of the existing urban forest. The inventory is the most time-consuming aspect of the master planning process.

3. *Tree lists.* The tree list is composed of natives, cultivars, and introductions which are most suited to the specific community.

Table 2.1.   Municipal Street Tree Master
Plan

Inventory
Analysis
Tree lists
Municipal environment
Aesthetics
Nurseries
Planting
Tree management
Pruning
Roots
IPM
Systemics
Forestry Department
Equipment
Contracting
Regulations
Public relations
Volunteers
Arbor Day
Tree City—USA
Accreditation

The trees should not require high maintenance or be susceptible to pests and disease. The list should be diversified. The street tree master plan should also indicate the sources of the trees. This information is expanded in Chap. 4.

4. *Municipal environment.*   An evaluation should be made of the municipal environment as it relates to municipal trees. The evaluation should look at soil, climate, existing forest trees, land use, aesthetic character, vegetative history, and other local information about trees. The evaluation should also look at the

municipal residents, their attitudes about trees, their willingness to pay for proper tree management, and their perception of the existing urban environment.

5. *Aesthetics.* Not only is the aesthetic value of a tree itself important, but also a tree should be selected that is best suited for the site in terms of its aesthetic value.

6. *Nurseries.* Should municipal street trees be grown in municipal nurseries, be purchased from nurseries, or gotten by a little bit of both? The answer is in Chap. 4.

7. *Tree planting.* The planting of a tree represents a community's future. Therefore, the best tree available should be carefully selected, located on a site where it will thrive, properly planted, watered, and given sufficient maintenance to ensure survival.

8. *Tree management.* The objectives of maintaining public trees include keeping trees in a safe condition, caring for the horticultural needs of a tree, and preserving a tree so that maximum benefits can be obtained. More information on this subject is found in Chap. 5.

9. *Pruning.* The pruning cycle should be systematic to decrease the cost per tree while increasing the safety and condition of the tree, thereby reducing service and storm damage requests. This effort results in a better public image and healthier trees.

10. *Roots.* Roots are probably the least known, most misunderstood, and least respected part of a tree. Because the roots of some tree varieties cause problems, all tree roots are abused. The root is vital in the proper, long-term development of healthy trees and a canopy of branches over the street.

11. *IPM.* Tree health care management should also consider disease and pest control through integrated pest management (IPM) techniques.

12. *Systemics.* Systemic tree injection is one technique that is both useful and controversial among forestry professionals. It is one of the tools available in an IPM program.

13. *Forestry Department.* To begin an analysis of the Forestry Department, a study should be made of the following items: number of trees to be maintained; frequency of maintenance or trimming cycle; work load per year; equipment and personnel required; budget for trimming, planting, removals, and administration; support services and contracts; employee training and morale; and other related items unique to each community. An evaluation should be made of the municipal forestry management program and a comparison made with

industry standards and practices in other communities. Identification of safe and economical work methods and procedures will enhance existing operations. Careful planning through the master plan will improve the cost-effectiveness of these operations. This subject is discussed in more detail in Chap. 6.

14. *Equipment.*   A general knowledge of the basic tools is essential for efficient street tree management. Tree pruning is the most costly operation in forestry department budgets. Mechanization in this area will reduce costs for the benefit of the entire department.

15. *Contracting.*   Contracting or the use of in-house labor should be chosen to ensure that tree maintenance is being performed at the lowest possible cost.

16. *Regulations.*   The municipal regulations pertaining to tree planting, tree management, and tree removals as well as other state and local regulations pertaining to street trees should be evaluated.

17. *Public relations.*   Public support comes in the form of the public's perception regarding the urban forestry program. Public support is necessary to obtain the funding necessary to pay for street tree management. Public support can be enhanced through a wide variety of public relations programs, explained in Chap. 7.

18. *Volunteers.*   All public support must be channeled through a Street Tree Advisory Board. This is a group of volunteers who establish the policies and recommendations that a forestry department must follow. Volunteers can also be used to assist in other aspects of the urban forestry program.

19. *Arbor Day.*   Very few other professions and interests have a holiday to commemorate them. Everyone involved in arboriculture should take advantage of this holiday. Involving children and elected officials in an Arbor Day Program can be very effective.

20. *Tree City—USA.*   This program, sponsored by the National Arbor Day Foundation, is a very popular program which draws attention to a city's urban forestry program. This, in turn, helps to promote continued success of urban forest management.

21. *Accreditation.*   This program, sponsored by the Society of Municipal Arborists, sets the highest standards of municipal arboriculture and awards to cities meeting these standards the title *Accredited Forestry Department.*

Typical master plans. (*Clockwise, from top left: Courtesy Wellesley, MA; Longview, OR; Oak Park, IL; Modesto, CA.*)

22. *Goal of them municipal street tree master plan.*   The goal is to create a realistic plan to achieve complete planting of every available site in the community. The planting should be done over a 20- to 50-year period and should be properly diversified. The plan should also indicate the maintenance goals so tree management can be completed in a cost-effective manner.

The street tree master plan should be developed under the supervision of a community's municipal arborist. The arborist will need assistance from volunteers, paid staff, or consultants. This assistance will be necessary to gather information, conduct evaluations, and do the actual report writing. Staff members might assist the arborist depending upon their work load and whether funds are available to pay for staff assistance. Another option is to utilize consultants who specialize in master plan preparation. The three largest firms that this author is familiar with are as follows: ACRT, Box 219, Kent, OH 44240-0219, phone 1-800-622-2562; Davey Resource Group, 18010 Skypark Circle, Suite 225, Irvine, CA 92714, phone 1-800-648-7337; and Asplundh Municipal Division, 168 Tamarack Circle, Montgomery Knoll, Skillman, NJ, 08558, phone 1-800-443-9558. There are many smaller landscape architectural or forestry consulting firms that can also provide this service, but their experience is very limited.

Follow-up

At least once a year, there should be a follow-up process to evaluate the work performance, planting progress, trees trimmed, inventory update, etc. The process will examine the work actually accomplished (compared to what was budgeted) and how closely the work met the established goals. Based upon this annual review, goals for the upcoming year may need to be revised and trimming programs or work schedules may need reevaluation.

Another follow-up item deals with the forestry department accreditation. Once a community has met all the requirements indicated in its municipal street tree master plan, it can apply for accreditation and probably win this honor.

SMA Forestry Department Accreditation Program

The Society of Municipal Arborists offers a program to provide accreditation to municipal forestry departments. The accreditation program is a nongovernment voluntary system of self-regulation which sets the highest standards for municipal arboriculture. Its purpose is to properly manage the urban forest, improve the citizens' health and welfare, enhance a community's beauty, and ensure the safety of the traveling public. The program evaluates each forestry department on the basis of its stated objectives as well as compliance with certain minimum standards.

The benefits of obtaining an accreditation certificate for the forestry department are many. For example, the SMA accreditation program acknowledges the work of the city foresters. This program tells them how well they are doing professionally. Accreditation is the endorsement and public recognition that the department has met all the formal requirements of arboricultural excellence in service, facilities, standards, and quality. The department is being judged by other municipal arborists (peers), and if the department can meet the accreditation standards, then it will know that it is one of the best forestry departments in the state and the United States and the municipal arborist will be individually recognized as a leader of one of the nation's best municipal forestry departments.

Accreditation also provides the community program with professional publicity. Besides press releases to local papers, cities that have received accreditation are featured nationally in *City Trees*, the journal of the Society of Municipal Arborists. Occasionally, announcements are made in other professional journals as well. In some situations, the community's liability is reduced because of accreditation and recognition that it meets the highest urban forestry standards in the nation. Accreditation also ensures the protection and safety of the community's residents by following the highest arboricultural standards.

The accreditation program standards are continually updated to ensure that a community is as current as possible regarding its municipal forestry program. The awarding of an Accredited Urban Forestry program is made at the annual meeting of the Society of Municipal Arborists and must be renewed every 5 years. All urban forestry programs are eligible, whether they are separate departments or a part of another department, as long as they meet the requirements for this program. A County Forestry Department Accreditation Program may also be available from the SMA. Membership in the SMA is not necessary.

The accreditation program consists of five parts:

1. A copy of the municipality's street tree master plan

2. A list of forestry-related characteristics of the applicant's municipality

3. Several requirements related to scheduling, planning work, and the forestry budget

4. Several requirements related to the qualifications of the municipal arborist

5. Several requirements related to the municipal forestry department

Specific requirements are detailed in Chap. 6 in the section pertaining to forestry department standards. The form takes about a day to write, provided all the necessary documents have been completed and the requirements have been met. It is an investment in planning that is very easily justified by any municipal official.

Sources

Phillips, Leonard E., Jr.: *Municipal Street Tree Master Planning,* Peabody, MA, 1981.
Street Tree Master Plan, Parks and Recreation Department, Modesto, CA, 1987.

3
Street Tree Inventory

Objectives

The management of any resource begins with an inventory of that resource. Street trees are no exception. A street tree inventory should be undertaken with the following objectives:

1. To count all street trees growing within the community boundaries by species and to determine their size, location, and condition

2. To record the observation of needs, such as pruning, fertilizing, and cable bracing or removal, and problems, such as insects, disease, aesthetic value, condition of the trees, shade canopy, insect damage, conflicts with utilities, and other evaluative data

3. To use the information gathered in programming tree care activities and to point out the need for additional plantings and alterations to the streetscape and the monetary value of the entire inventory

4. Any other purpose that would be useful to the municipal arborist and a community

When a city is planning to change its image through a major tree planting effort and set up or revitalize its forestry program, the city will usually consider undertaking an inventory so proper planning is done. Once these data have been obtained, they can be organized to serve as a useful source of information for the ongoing tree care program. The inventory can be used to justify the municipal tree budget for popular planting programs as well as for maintenance programs. The inventory information, when properly used, can decrease a community's liability for tree damage. The inventory also lends itself to monthly and yearly reports of completed work on trees in the inventory. The inventory is also desirable when a new tree planting or tree maintenance program is being established. It can also enhance a community's eligibility for a grant. The inventory allows the municipal arborist the opportunity to make intelligent responses to calls from the public. This public service is appealing to administrators. The information in the inventory is a valuable asset to the municipal arborist as she or he provides a diverse tree planting population and establishes certain maintenance needs. It can also be used to project heavy periods of removal, required pruning, and planting needs. The inventory is also valuable in assessing the monetary value of the community's trees. It is also used to analyze maintenance costs and other costs requested by city officials.

Once the guidelines have been established, every street tree location should be mapped on a grid and at a scale convenient for the arborist and the community to depict the overall tree canopy of the community. Each shade tree is shown on the map by using various symbols. The symbols represent the actual size of the tree and whether the tree is coniferous or deciduous. A brief review of these maps enables one to quickly determine if an area is well foliated and if the foliage provides shade cover over the street. Also apparent are the size, number, mixture, and relative locations of the trees. The first six illustrations in this chapter illustrate how four communities have mapped their trees.

The information collected on each tree varies according to the needs of the arborist, but it can include what is shown in Tables 3-1 and 3-2.

All the information being gathered should be useful in establishing a meaningful tree planting program. For example, the utility information will indicate that low trees can be planted under the wires or shallow-rooted trees cannot be planted beside the sidewalks. Maintenance needs can be recorded and projected if the inventory information is sufficient. Before an inventory is undertaken, however, the municipal arborist should evaluate what reports, graphs, charts, maps, and other information are required for maximum utilization of the inventory. According to consultants who provide services to municipalities, a common list of inventory information to be collected is shown in Table 3-3 in decreasing order of importance to the municipality.

Inventory Computerization

The most important reason for computerizing the street tree inventory is to make the inventory information more readily

Table 3-1. Data Collection

Tree location
Street name: actual or code name
House number: actual house, lot number, assumed number noted on plans, opposite, median
Tree or cell number: See previous illustrations for example.
Width of tree lawn: actual in feet, or none, or attached to lawn
Presence and condition of sidewalk: yes, none, material, condition (excellent, poor)
Map number: depends upon local mapping system
Management unit: important in large cities, wards, maintenance areas
Distance from curb: actual in feet
House setback: approximate in feet (to determine available planting space)

Species identification
Name: in scientific, common, variety, cultivar, or code
Vacant: planting site, stump, unacceptable site, shrubs growing

Physical conditions
Crown development: full and balanced, unbalanced, thin
Trunk diameter: in inches or 6-inch intervals, forked, clump
Value: in dollars and according to appraisal formula
Tree crown spread: in feet or 5-foot intervals
Trunk condition: sound, missing bark, hollow
Biomass: dynamic—amount of tree mass canopy; static—wood portion no longer growing
Height: in feet or 10-foot intervals
Life expectancy: 10-year intervals, time left
Forest or hedge of trees: consistently count as one item or individual trees

Environmental conditions
Underground utilities: location within 5 feet
Overhead utilities: yes or no
Irrigation needs: if important

Table 3-1. Data Collection (Continued)

Environmental conditions

Soils: correlated to tree needs

Land use: commercial, industrial, residential, open space, institution

Pollution: heavy traffic, dense population

Growing space: small, medium, large

Maintenance classifications

Condition codes: see Table 3-2

Pruning: needs, roots, deformity, multiple trunk, safety, routine, shape, clearance

Injury: insects, diseases, needs attention

Miscellaneous remarks: location such as spacing, shaded, or poor location; form and shape, such as good, poor, deformity, multiple trunks, etc.; suggested treatments such as insect control, pruning, removal, fertilize, cabling, aerate, or water

Table 3-2. Condition Codes

The condition of trees may vary from 0 to 100 percent according to the ISA appraisal formula:

Class I, 90 to 100 percent, excellent   Trees in this class are judged to be exceptional trees and possess the best qualities of the species. All have excellent form and very minor maintenance problems and are growing in a location which will enable them to achieve a full mature shape.

Class II, 70 to 89 percent, good   Trees in this class are judged to be good trees which with proper maintenance can be brought into very good condition for the future. They are growing in interference with utility lines or are overcrowded or have insect problems or nutritional deficiencies.

Class III, 50 to 69 percent, fair   Most trees in this group have the following problems: large dead limbs with as much as one-half of the tree already dead; large cavities; drastic deformities; girdling roots; severe insect or pathological problems.

Class IV, 1 to 49 percent, poor   Trees in this group are either dead or in very poor condition with irreversible problems. Trees in this group will have to be removed in the near future.

Table 3-3. Useful Inventory Information

Inventory information	Most likely use
Street name and house number	Crews use this information to find a tree and to be able to answer resident inquiries about this tree over the phone.
Geographical area of city	Used for recording systematic trimming, scheduling tree management within a subarea, and inspections.
Multiple trees on one property	Used in identifying trees in the field.
Species	Used for treatment of diseases and insects and for planting decisions.
Diameter	Useful for estimating budgets.
Maintenance needs	Needs that can be listed for crews.
Blockside information	List of all trees on a street. Useful for systematic maintenance.
Condition	Used for determining species performance.
Overhead wires	Useful for selecting trees to be planted.
Planting sites	Useful for telling the total number of trees that should be planted.
Other maintenance needs—girdling roots, insects, diseases, fertilizer, cabling, aeration, and watering	Useful, if these operations are done, for determining the budget.
Missing addresses	Useful for crew to know that the tree is on a vacant lot.

Table 3-3. Useful Inventory Information (Continued)

Inventory information	Most likely use
Other site characteristics: width of tree lawn, distance to curb, house setback, and distance to adjacent trees	Used in aiding selection of species for planting.
Location rating	Useful for estimation of tree value.
Exact location of street trees	Useful for spatial analysis.

available than it would be with other record storage systems and to enable the contents to be analyzed. This allows the municipal tree department an easy opportunity for answering complaints and questions from the public about any tree in the city. The computerization of the inventory will also benefit the maintenance operations by describing any tree in the inventory; by improving the scheduling of routine maintenance, the spraying operations, leaf pickup programs, etc; and by making overall improvements in the community tree care program. Administrative duties such as scheduling for more efficient use of resources, budget justifications, and preparations of annual reports will be reduced and simplified by the use of a computerized tree inventory system. Use of species and tree age, determined by the diameter information in the tree inventory, enables the arborist to project years of extra-high trimming and removal costs followed by high planting costs; for a young tree population, the maintenance costs will be needed in trimming. Trees properly pruned while young will experience moderate pruning needs during the mature years.

Another reason for having an inventory is the statistical analysis that is available. The statistics cover the number of trees, species, and trees by species plus the reporting history and work demands. Finally, computerization will ease any planning operations which might require the selection of species for tree planting programs and landscape planting plans. Planning capability can also be useful for projecting maintenance costs such as spraying and pruning needs.

The computer program compiles the inventory list of trees. The program lists the trees according to street address, map number, and tree number; the location of the tree and distance from the curb; house setback; tree species; caliper, tree condition, and monetary value. The computer program stores the data and keeps a history of the tree by incorporating the details of the completed work, such as trimming, spraying, or removal, or annual tree growth. It can recall data according to the street and number; tree condition; distance from the curb; tree caliper; tree value; tree species; tree work needed; reference number; and combinations of the above. This allows for periodic summaries to be produced which indicate number of removals, miles of street tree pruning, etc. A maintenance distribution report will provide number of removals, trimming, planting, etc., which enables the arborist to justify the budget before the city council. A typical report generated by a computer program is illustrated in Table 3-4. This report comes from the city of Toledo.

At one time, communities developed their own programs to store and retrieve inventory information. Today, however, several preprogrammed computerized systems for automating the storage, retrieval, and analysis of street trees have been developed for municipalities. There are also several companies and firms which offer inventory services to municipalities. Generally, the cost of using these firms and their programs is much less than the cost to a community for developing its own system. Furthermore, the inventory costs can sometimes be combined with a major municipal tree planting initiative. Some of the largest and most well-known firms include ACRT and Davey Resource Group, mentioned in Chap. 2. The basic programs, inventory, and other services vary somewhat in sophistication as well as cost.

Data Collection

Once a decision has been made regarding whether to proceed with an inventory, what information is to be collected, and whether the information is to be computerized, the next major decision concerns how the information is to be collected. If volunteers or municipal laborers are to be used, they need training. If a consultant is to be hired, sufficient funds must be available, and the entire inventory process can be done as a single contract or in small components.

The next decision deals with collecting the information. Should paper charts be developed which provide an outline of the information to be collected? This will then require keypunching the information into the computer. If portable data collection devices are used, the information can be easily and quickly transferred to the computer. The device will also act somewhat as an accuracy check if a nonexistent species is incorrectly entered. Operating the data collection device may also require special training. Next, a decision has to be made regarding transportation. Should the survey be done from a windshield tour or by foot? Windshield inventories, which may be done quickly and are useful for statistical

Table 3-4. Sample Species Information

Common name	0–3	3–6	6–12	12–18	18–24	24–30	30–36	36	Total trees	Percent of population
Crepe Myrtle	734	95	11	0	0	0	0	0	840	11.1
Callery Pear	168	201	133	4	0	0	0	0	506	6.7
Camphor	225	134	93	6	4	3	0	0	465	6.2
Modesto Ash	29	50	135	111	72	27	18	2	444	5.9
Fruitless Mulberry	29	27	75	169	80	22	3	0	405	5.4
Sweetgum	49	45	175	41	5	2	0	0	317	4.2
Purple Leaf Plum	62	175	54	1	1	0	0	0	293	3.9
Chinese Pistache	193	46	31	1	0	0	0	0	271	3.6
Oleander	37	54	104	5	3	0	0	0	203	2.7
Grecian Laurel	77	80	26	1	0	0	0	0	184	2.4
Italian Cypress	67	90	11	0	3	0	0	0	171	2.3
Evergreen Pear	33	105	16	3	0	0	0	0	157	2.1
California Sycamore	2	13	27	52	31	23	8	0	156	2.1
Raywood Ash	137	4	1	1	0	0	0	0	143	1.9
Southern Magnolia	46	59	29	0	0	0	0	0	134	1.8
Mediterranean Fan Palm	15	43	20	23	15	7	5	6	134	1.8
Chinese Elm	17	44	26	8	0	2	0	1	98	1.3
Bottlebrush	52	33	11	1	0	0	0	0	97	1.3
Japanese Photinia	73	21	0	0	0	0	0	0	94	1.2
Arborvitae	36	49	8	0	0	0	0	0	93	1.2
Monterey Pine	7	29	35	21	0	1	0	0	93	1.2
Japanese Privet	40	37	15	0	0	0	0	0	92	1.2
Chinaberry	3	1	15	23	21	18	8	2	91	1.2

London Plane Tree	1	0	32	24	24	4	2	0	87	1.1
Japanese Black Pine	37	39	10	0	0	0	0	0	86	1.1
Flowering Cherry	46	32	4	1	0	0	0	0	83	1.1
Canary Island Pine	45	12	17	5	1	1	0	0	81	1.1
Chinese Hackberry	60	10	4	0	0	0	0	0	74	1.0
Olive	22	18	20	7	2	0	0	0	69	0.9
English Walnut	5	3	23	19	9	3	2	1	65	0.9
Stone Pine	11	16	23	9	1	2	1	0	63	0.8

SOURCE: ACRT.

Large branch of sugar maple tree frames the view of the town square.

purposes, are not accurate enough for compiling a complete inventory and for maintenance records. Inventory by foot means that the survey is accurate and detailed, but it will take considerable time to complete.

The success of the entire inventory data collection process is the result of excellent training, supervision, quality control, and input from the municipal forestry personnel. Success is also ensured if all work is entered into the inventory system as the work is completed. Reinventory can be done periodically. Reinventory is also an option which allows the inventory updates to be a budget item.

A partial inventory may be useful as a trial run to provide the estimated number of trees and maintenance requirements; from this, a budget can be developed to prepare a complete inventory. A statistically accurate, quick inventory to establish a data base can be done. The procedures for this rapid inventory are explained in Chap. 8. However, to consider anything less than a 100 percent inventory complete would be faulty reasoning. This information cannot be used from one year to the next or as a base for a working document. This is because trees are maintained individually and work performed on one tree is not necessarily needed on the next one.

The key to success is to determine what information is needed for each individual municipality and how often this information will be used. Each community is different and requires different street tree management techniques. Therefore, street tree inventory programs should be adapted to meet the needs of the individual community.

Using the Street Tree Inventory

The inventory provides a base of information which should be used by the municipal arborist to analyze the tree population. The information can be manipulated by computer to produce lists of trees according to:

1. Tree species and number of trees per species. This information can be summarized and used to calculate species diversity. An example of this information is shown in Table 3-4.

2. Location within the right-of-way. This information will be used during routine scheduled pruning operations.

3. Size, which can also be used to calculate a functional age (young, intermediate, mature, old), maintenance needs, and mortality rates.

4. The number of stumps and vacancies available for future plantings.

5. The value of the entire tree population as well as the value of trees by species, size, etc. (The value is especially significant in justifying a maintenance budget.)

6. Conditions which indicate pruning needs to improve the tree; safety pruning for pedestrians and vehicles; clearance pruning for signs, lights, and traffic control; mortality rates, etc.

7. Training small trees to grow into specimens through proper pruning techniques.

8. Damage caused to sidewalks.

9. Removal needs according to priorities (urgent, short-term, and long-term).

10. Height, another function of forest age.

The inventory information can also be used as a work scheduling system. The software package should allow for periodic summaries to be produced which indicate the number of removals, miles of street tree pruning, etc. A maintenance distribution report will provide the number of removals, trimming, planting, etc., which enables the arborist to justify the budget before the city council. The work records can be applied against standards to measure performance. Performance standards are prepared from an average of the work done by crews during a given period. This information is computerized by tree diameter and by species to prepare a table of standards. This information is then used to compare actual work with the standards. Items that are measured include tree work, such as trimming, planting, removal, etc.; travel time; stump removal; downtime; storm damage, etc. The summary can also be produced by crews and used for management counseling for employees. The summary can also be produced according to specific locations within the municipality. More information on performance standards is given in the pruning section of Chap. 5.

Over the long term, the record-keeping system will keep the inventory up to date. Checking the inventory every 5 years will also assist in managing the urban forest. The records will indicate how the street trees are doing; which species are growing well; which species require heavy maintenance; which locations, soils, and other site conditions affect tree growth. And the records will provide documentation as to where, and for what purpose, maintenance funds have been spent. The goal of this exercise is to provide guidance for future management efforts and improved planting guidelines. The reinventory will also check the records and accuracy for the past 5 years.

Below is a drawing of several street trees that illustrates the use of blockside information. In the drawing, the shaded areas with a number in them represent the trees. Boxes with an address in them represent buildings with addresses. Four streets are also represented in the drawing: First Street, Second Street, Main Street, and Vine Street. The table below lists the blockside information for all eight trees in the drawing.

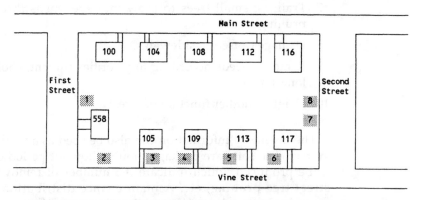

Tree #	Address and Street Name	Blockside Information		
		On Street	From Street	To Street
1	558 First Street	First Street	Main Street	Vine Street
2	558 First Street	Vine Street	First Street	Second Street
3	105 Vine Street	Vine Street	First Street	Second Street
4	109 Vine Street	Vine Street	First Street	Second Street
5	113 Vine Street	Vine Street	First Street	Second Street
6	117 Vine Street	Vine Street	First Street	Second Street
7	117 Vine Street	Second Street	Vine Street	Main Street
8	117 Vine Street	Second Street	Vine Street	Main Street

Description of blockside information. (*Courtesy ACRT.*)

Any property can be divided into a seven by seven grid. Each box in the drawing below is called a cell. When dealing with street trees, we are primarily interested with trees across the front of the property. Therefore, the cells numbered 1-7 below are the most commonly used cell numbers. Cell numbers 8-24 are used to describe trees located on the side of a lot, or the rear of a lot.

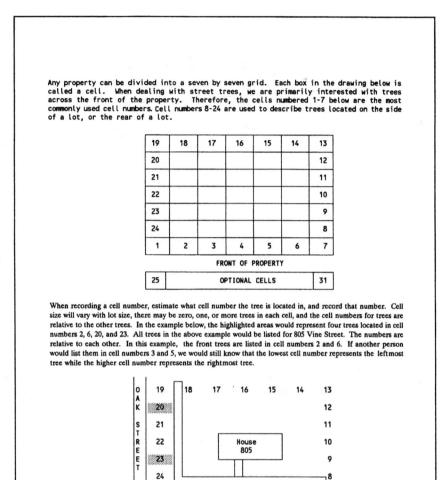

When recording a cell number, estimate what cell number the tree is located in, and record that number. Cell size will vary with lot size, there may be zero, one, or more trees in each cell, and the cell numbers for trees are relative to the other trees. In the example below, the highlighted areas would represent four trees located in cell numbers 2, 6, 20, and 23. All trees in the above example would be listed for 805 Vine Street. The numbers are relative to each other. In this example, the front trees are listed in cell numbers 2 and 6. If another person would list them in cell numbers 3 and 5, we would still know that the lowest cell number represents the leftmost tree while the higher cell number represents the rightmost tree.

Cell number concept for location of multiple trees at one address. (*Courtesy ACRT.*)

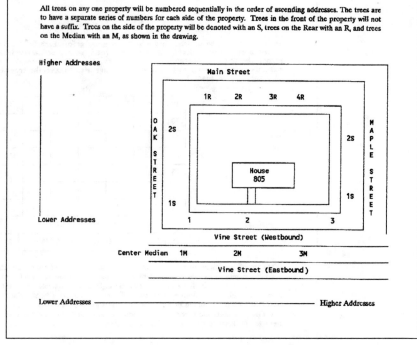

All trees on any one property will be numbered sequentially in the order of ascending addresses. The trees are to have a separate series of numbers for each side of the property. Trees in the front of the property will not have a suffix. Trees on the side of the property will be denoted with an S, trees on the Rear with an R, and trees on the Median with an M, as shown in the drawing.

Tree numbering for multiple trees at one address. (*Courtesy ACRT.*)

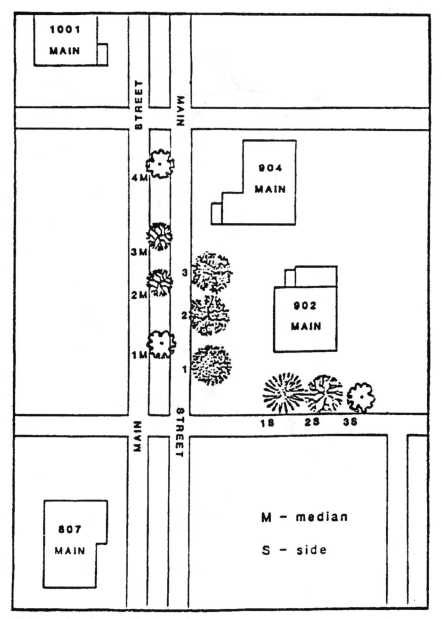

Scheme for the numbering of trees in Newark's street tree inventory.

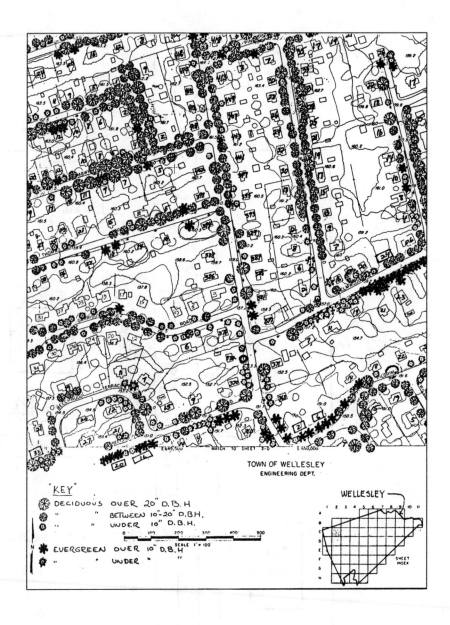

TOWN OF WELLESLEY
ENGINEERING DEPT.

"KEY"

⊛ DECIDUOUS OVER 20" D.B.H

⊙ "   "   BETWEEN 10"-20" D.B.H.

∘ "   "   UNDER 10" D.B.H.

❋ EVERGREEN OVER 10" D.B.H

✳ "   "   UNDER "   "

0   100   200   300   400'   500
SCALE 1" = 100'

WELLESLEY

SHEET INDEX

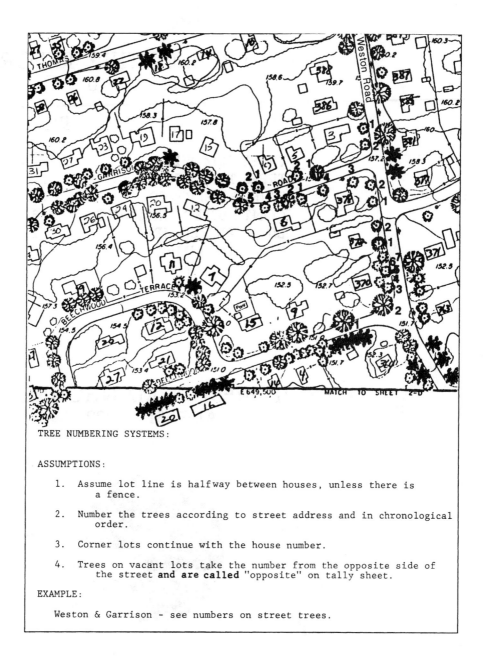

TREE NUMBERING SYSTEMS:

ASSUMPTIONS:

1. Assume lot line is halfway between houses, unless there is a fence.

2. Number the trees according to street address and in chronological order.

3. Corner lots continue with the house number.

4. Trees on vacant lots take the number from the opposite side of the street **and are called** "opposite" on tally sheet.

EXAMPLE:

Weston & Garrison - see numbers on street trees.

FORESTRY MONTHLY REPORT
AUGUST - 1990

PROJECT	UNITS
TREES REMOVED	204
TREES TRIMMED	115
STUMPS REMOVED	105
CONTRACTED TRIMMING	32
LIMBS PICKED UP	27
HANGING LIMBS	23

FORESTRY MANHOURS
AUGUST - 1990

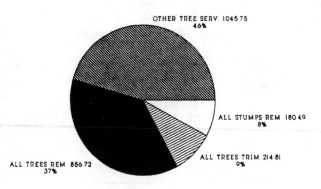

FORESTRY PERFORMANCE
AUGUST - 1990

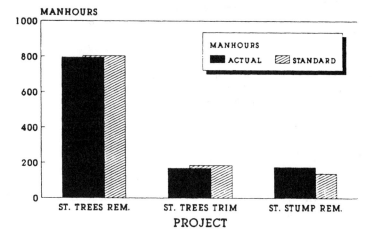

OTHER TREE SERV. MANHOURS
AUGUST - 1990

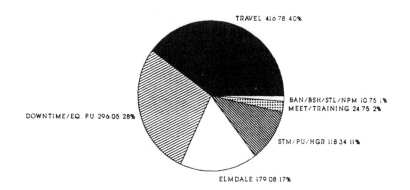

Sources

ACRT: *Street Tree Inventory and Urban Forestry Management Plan for Hanford, CA*, Kent, OH, 1991.

Joehlin, Ken, and Pat O'Brien: "The Tools for Urban Forestry Management," *City Trees*, May/June 1991, p. 16.

Miller, Robert W.: *Urban Forestry—Planning and Managing Urban Greenspaces*, Prentice-Hall, Englewood Cliffs, NJ, 1988.

Phillips, Leonard E., Jr.: "Municipal Street Tree Inventory," *City Trees*, November 1982, p. 9.

Sacksteader, C. J., and H. D. Gerhold: *A Guide to Urban Tree Inventory Systems*, USDA Forest Service, Research Paper 43, 1979.

Sudal, F. S., and A. L. Zach: *Urban Tree Management in Newark*, City of Newark, NJ, 1986.

Endnote

Special thanks for technical assistance to Kenneth Joehlin (ACRT Inc.), Robert Carroll (Davey Resource Group), and Chris Carlson (Kent State University—Salem).

4

Recommended Street Trees

Ideal street trees should live at least 50 years and preferably 100; they should have few pest problems; they should be disease-resistant; they should tolerate the local urban environment and pollution problems; they should tolerate deicing materials such as road salt; they should not be susceptible to dieback; they should have the ability to be upbranched; they should have good structure; they should not be dropping fruit; they should be hardy; they should not have brittle branches or anchorage problems; they should not have surface roots, especially near sidewalks; they should tolerate local soils; they should have seasonal color; they should need little maintenance; and above all, they should be beautiful year-round.

Tree Selection Process

However, since one perfect tree does not exist, tree selections should be made by using the best trees that we do have. There are several steps necessary to establish a list of plant material most suited to a specific community. The first step consists of collecting a list of native and hardy plant material. This list is modified by removing those materials which, experience has indicated, do poorly in local roadside or urban conditions. Then the tree list is supplemented with "native cultivars," which are improved varieties of the native species in terms of disease and insect pest resistance and enhanced visual qualities. Then introductions which have become established and tolerant of growing conditions in the community are added to the list. These introductions are included only to provide a well-rounded selection and sufficient number of species for proper diversification. Remove from this list trees with high maintenance costs, surface roots, intolerance to storms, and undesirable fruiting habits.

To further refine the plant material selection process, it is advisable to compare the selections with what other authorities have recommended. This information comes from books, local universities, or extension services. Local nurseries can be used to determine what species are available and what are recommended. Table 4-1, Ideal Trees for Downtown Plantings, illustrates the trees recommended by this author. Table 4-2, a list of undesirable street trees, is simply a list of trees that should not be planted in an urban or street landscape. Appendix B, Recommended Trees from Various Cities, at the end of this book illustrates tree selections from municipalities that have superior tree management programs.

Once a list of trees such as Table 4-1 has been compiled, it should remain open so the municipal arborist can add new trees as he or she finds them or as they become developed and can delete undesirable trees if experience reveals problems. The master plan should also include a list of trees such as those in Table 4-2 that are unacceptable in the community.

Diversification Formula

The diversification formula has been developed to prevent overdependence on a single genus such as American Chestnut or American Elm. The diversification formula was established by the International Society of Arboriculture and is now an accepted standard throughout the United States. The formula is defined as a planting plan containing no more than 10 percent of one family and 5 percent of one species.

Therefore, for every 100 trees planted, care should be taken that no more than 10 trees are planted of any one family, such as pines, and no more than 5 trees of any one species, such as Red Oak. The city of Lansing, Michigan, has a diversification policy which states, "No tree will be planted next to a tree of the same species, and at least four genus will be planted on a street."

The diversification formula should be carried one step further. It should be applied to the existing street tree inventory so that dependence on a single species from previous or natural plantings will not be carried forward into future plantings. The diversification formula was set up so that if 3 percent of a city's tree population were Red Oak and a disease or insect killed them all, then 97 percent of the trees would still remain. The American Elm comprised as much as 50 percent of the urban tree population before Dutch Elm disease (DED) devastated the landscape across North America. The diversification formula is difficult to use in zones 2 and 3 and in other places where the number of trees is severely restricted due to soil or climatic conditions.

Table 4-1. Ideal Trees for Downtown Plantings

Scientific name	Common name
Zone 2	
Sorbus hupehensis 'Coral Fire'	Coral Fire Mountain Ash
Zone 3	
Acer platanoides 'Cleveland'	Cleveland Norway Maple
Acer platanoides 'Summershade'	Summershade Norway Maple
Acer rubrum 'Red Sunset'	Red Sunset Red Maple
Acer saccharum 'Green Mountain'	Green Mountain Maple
Celtis occidentalis 'Prairie Pride'	Prairie Pride Hackberry
Cladrastis lutea	Yellowwood
Fraxinus excelsior 'Hessei'	Hesse European Ash
Fraxinus pennsylvanica 'Summit'	Summit Ash
Ostrya virginiana	Hop Hornbeam
Quercus rubra	Red Oak
Syringa reticulata 'Ivory Silk'	Ivory Silk Tree Lilac
Zone 4	
Acer campestre 'Queen Elizabeth'	Queen Elizabeth Hedge Maple
Acer freemani 'Celebration'	Celebration Maple
Acer rubrum 'Karpick'	Karpick Red Maple
Acer saccharum 'Endowment Columnar'	Endowment Columnar Sugar Maple
Acer tartaricum	Tartarian Maple
Carpinus betulus fastigiata	Pyramidal European Hornbeam
Cercidiphyllum japonicum	Katsura tree
Chionanthus virginicus	Fringe tree
Corylus colurna	Turkish Hazelnut
Crataegus phaenopyrum	Washington Hawthorn
Eucommia ulmoides	Hardy Rubber tree
Ginkgo biloba 'Princeton Sentry'	Princeton Sentry Ginkgo
Gleditsia triacanthos inermis 'Shademaster'	Shademaster Honeylocust
Ilex verticillata 'Winter Red'	Winter Red Winterberry
Liquidambar styraciflua 'Moraine'	Moraine Sweet Gum
Maclura pomifera inermis 'Park'	Park Osage Orange
Malus 'Centurion'	Centurion Crabapple
Malus 'Harvest Gold'	Harvest Gold Crabapple

Table 4-1. Ideal Trees for Downtown Plantings (Continued)

Zone 4	
Malus 'Sugar Tyme'	Sugar Tyme Crabapple
Nyssa sylvatica	Black Tupelo
Prunus sargentii	Sargent Cherry
Pyrus calleryana 'Aristocrat'	Aristocrat Pear
Pyrus calleryana 'Redspire'	Redspire Pear
Sophora japonica 'Regent'	Regent Scholartree
Tilia tomentosa 'Sterling Silver'	Sterling Silver Linden

Zone 5	
Acer griseum	Paperbark Maple
Betula nigra 'Heritage'	Heritage Birch
Cornus kousa 'Summer Stars'	Summer Stars Dogwood
Magnolia stellata 'Galaxy'	Galaxy Magnolia
Oxydendrum arboreum	Sourwood
Parrotia persica	Persian Parrotia
Plantanus acerfolia 'Bloodgood'	Bloodgood London Plane
Zelkova serrata 'Green Vase'	Green Vase Zelkova

Zone 6	
Celtis occidentalis 'Magnifica'	Magnifica Hackberry
Cornus florida 'President Ford'	President Ford Variegated Dogwood
Franklinia altamaha	Franklin tree

Zone 7	
Magnolia grandiflora	Southern Magnolia
Vitex agnus-castus	Chase tree

Table 4-2. Undesirable Street Trees

Scientific name	Common name	Comments
Acer negundo	Boxelder	Weak wood; aggressive, shallow roots
Acer saccharinum	Silver Maple	Weak wood; aggressive, shallow roots
Ailanthus altissima	Tree of Heaven	Weak wood
Albizia Julilbrissin	Silktree/Mimosa	Messy, excessive insects and diseases
Catalpa species	Catalpa	Messy, weak wood

Table 4-2. Undesirable Street Trees (Continued)

Scientific name	Common name	Comments
Celtis occidentalis	Hackberry	Insects and diseases, surface roots, no ornamental value
Fraxinus velutina glabra	Modesto Ash	Sidewalk problems
Ginkgo biloba—female	Ginkgo	Smelly fruit
Gymnocladus dioica	Kentucky Coffee tree	Messy fruit
Liquidambar styraciflua	Sweet Gum	Sidewalk problems, messy fruit
Maclura pomifera	Osage Orange	Invasive, thorns, sidewalk problems
Morus species	Mulberry	Sidewalk problems, messy twigs and fruit
Populus deltoides	Cottonwood	Weak, short-lived, cotton problems
Populus nigra `Italia'	Lombardy Poplar	Insects and diseases, weak wood
Populus tremulodies	Quaking Aspen	Insects and diseases, weak wood
Quercus palustris	Pin Oak	Chlorosis in alkaline soils
Rhus species	Sumac	Weak wood
Robinia	Black Locust	Insects and diseases, messy twigs, storm damage
Salix species	Willow	Sidewalk problems, messy twigs, insects and diseases, weak wood, invades drains and sewers
Ulmus americana	American Elm	Insects and diseases
Ulmus pumila	Siberian Elm	Insects and diseases, weak wood, storm damage
Evergreens	Evergreens	Shade streets in winter

Once the tree planting list is established, it can be used to match the trees to the planting sites in accordance with municipal regulations, utilities, structures, climate, and other urban and environmental factors. The size of the tree at maturity should also be taken into consideration when a tree is located at its permanent site.

Municipal Environment

The environmental situation in the community must be determined in order to match a proposed list of trees to specific locations. The environmental situation is ascertained by conducting an analysis of the soil; the existing, native, and planted vegetation; utility locations; subways; legal restrictions; sidewalks; signs; vents; awnings; environmental hazards; the plant hardiness zone; and the overall weather as well as any microclimatic conditions. The community's environment must be examined in terms of the tree's environmental preferences described above in the detailed description of trees selected for the community.

Of all the environmental considerations, soil analysis is one of the most important for growing healthy trees. The soils map should be prepared to show the basic generalized categories of soils, such as moist soils, dry soils, mixed soils, etc., as they apply to the individual community. Each site should also be examined regarding drainage, soil properties and type, pH, and salt residue; and perhaps a soil test should be done.

In addition to an evaluation and analysis of the existing street trees, an evaluation must be made of the existing forested areas of the community and, if possible, a native vegetation history of the community's forests must be prepared. The important features to be studied include the diversification of species, tree health, age of the forests, and other conditions unique to the community. This information, when added to the inventory information, will prevent overplanting of certain species common to the region. The lack of certain trees may also indicate what will not survive in a region.

A study of land uses should be made in combination with an analysis of the existing street tree inventory, to establish the aesthetic character of the neighborhoods or areas within a community. A land-use map should be prepared to show generalized land uses in categories which are simplistically defined. For example, commercial and industrial areas are heavily urbanized and are generally devoid of any significant, healthy trees; institutional and open-space areas contain large areas of native vegetation where natural succession and biological processes are occurring; and residential areas generally contain a wide diversity of species, lot sizes, home sizes, and available space, which is critical for determining tree habitats.

To ensure proper growth and minimum damage to trees, other factors to be considered include the analysis of road salt accumulation, high wind sites, excessive sun, excessive shade, natural-gas trunk lines, and sites subject to frequent mechanical injury.

Upon completion of a list of hardy street trees, which will thrive in the community, the environmental preferences of each tree species must be determined. The list of selected trees should be analyzed, shifted around, and matched to soil preferences and environmental tolerances. This information can be obtained from any source which describes trees in detail. The tree lists should be grouped into the same groups described above. The purpose of this study is to establish lists of trees that match community sites.

The municipal environmental analysis should also consider the human environment and its impact on street trees. For example, do the residents have a positive feeling toward trees, or are the trees just considered a nuisance every fall? Do the residents complain to their local political leaders and insist that existing trees be cut down? Or do they support major tree planting initiatives?

What does municipal forestry budget look like? Does it exist? Is it the first to be cut in tight economies? Or does it remain intact with strong support from all areas of the community? There is also a perceived correlation between the abundance of forests surrounding the community and the respect for trees within the community. For example, cities in the middle of the forest seldom have respect for trees along the city streets. The reverse is often true in cities where few trees exist except the precious few growing along the streets.

The socioeconomic condition of the community or area within a large city in general can also affect tree value. Poor areas and cities seldom have extra funds available to plant trees while affluent communities will plant as many trees as the land can hold. Trees increase real estate value, so only the high-income person can afford a home in a community with lots of trees. Whether planting many trees in poor areas in an attempt to raise real estate values and improve the attitudes of the residents will succeed is subject to much speculation.

Vandalism and respect for trees are another major consideration in evaluating the human environment of a tree planting site. Small trees cost less but are often vandalized. Large trees, which are vandal-resistant, are not affordable. Using potential vandals, local youths, and volunteers to help plant and maintain local trees will often help develop respect and longevity for trees.

All these human factors should be considered in determining the scope, size, and success of the urban forest.

All this information is brought together in a street tree planting plan. The different areas according to soils, land uses, vegetation patterns, and environmental hazards are combined on one map or on a chart of cross-reference to illustrate different tree planting areas; and each area is assigned a list of trees most appropriate for that area. When tree selections are being made from this list, consideration must be given to any environmental hazards at any individual location so that trees most tolerant of this hazard are used. The specific site should also be examined to determine the area available for future growth and any unrecorded restrictions which might affect the long-term health of the tree.

Many tree planting programs might also define more specifically where and how trees can be planted. These items might include the number of trees per lot; location in relation to the street, walk, and land uses; and location with regard to utilities, sight distance, and other trees. Some master plans might also include notes or details about tree planting techniques unique to a particular community.

Tree Selections

Dutch Elm disease was responsible for the development of both the diversification formula and a new breed of urban trees. When the DED outbreak began, research was started to breed resistant trees. This effort reinforced similar efforts made many years ago, to counteract the effects of the American Chestnut blight. The National Arboretum began by developing several new trees for use in urban areas. Nurseries and universities in North America also joined in the effort to breed new trees and develop selections of trees which have the characteristics of desirable street trees.

Table 4-1 is a list of 50 trees that should do well in downtown situations. These trees have thick or waxy leaves to tolerate drought or have genetic resistance to pests and tolerance to pollution. Some effort has also been made to select trees which will not be severely damaged by storms or road salt. However, this should not be considered as a guarantee of storm and salt resistance. Since this list represents only the hardiest of urban trees for downtown or sidewalk plantings, the municipal arborist should supplement the list with other trees for planting in parks, residential areas, etc., to achieve proper diversification. Table 4-1 is organized according to hardiness zone, and Table 4-2 indicates trees which should not be planted in densely populated areas. It is important to stress that these trees are, in the author's opinion, the best 50 urban trees. Every expert should be able to generate her or his own list of "best trees."

There may be other species that are unacceptable due to local conditions such as hardiness, overabundance, not adaptable to local soils, or local pest or disease problems. These species should be added to the list of undesirable trees by the municipal arborist. Both lists (ideal trees and undesirable trees) should be written for the local community and published in the street tree master plan and tree planting regulations.

Small trees are used under the wires and large trees are used over them.

Tree Aesthetics

Aesthetics and function should also work together to determine the selection of an urban tree species. What is the purpose of the tree in the landscape? Is it to screen views, provide shade, enhance the aesthetics, form a promenade, enclose a space, or improve the site and environments?

Definitely shaped trees and ornamental flowering or fruiting trees should be carefully selected and located to avoid distractions to drivers while at the same time providing an accent denoting a special view or structure. The tree itself can become the focal point through spectacular flowers or fall foliage. Trees should be used to frame pictures in the landscape, to hide objectionable views, and to supplement the existing vegetation. They can also assist in defining the edge of the roadway and enhancing spatial qualities. Spacing between trees should vary from 30 to 100 feet to create a naturalized appearance; thus if one tree dies or is removed, it does not spoil the continuity of the planting. Trees need sufficient unpaved areas for maximum health and vigor. They should be allowed to develop into perfect specimens and true representatives of their species. They should not be dangerously close to traffic in the street and, whenever possible, should be planted behind the sidewalk to achieve as much growing environment as allowable.

A tree's shape or form is an important consideration when a tree is chosen for a particular site. For example, trees can be shaped as illustrated on the next few pages:

Columnar trees provide a vertical line which is severe and gives a feeling of height.

Fastigate trees have strongly ascending branches, and the tree is very narrow.

Rounded trees have crowns which can provide dense shade.

Irregular trees provide interest and contrast to architecture because of the variable outline.

Weeping trees provide a unique form which leads attention from the tree to the ground.

Aristocrat Pear becomes the focal point in this landscape.

Vase-shaped trees form high branches which provide usable space underneath the tree. Trees of this shape also blend well with architecture and are most compatible with other shapes.

Pyramidal trees provide strong contrast and are difficult to blend in with other shapes. They accentuate spired architecture and are an excellent shape for the specimen location.

Colors also require consideration when a tree is chosen. Tree colors come from the seasonal flowers, fruits, and leaves; the winter bark color; and the summer leaf.

Tree textures vary from the very fine leaf of the honeylocust, for example, to the coarse-textured sycamore. The fine textures are light and airy, complement smooth architectural surfaces, and blend with the hard texture and dominant smooth surfaces. Coarse textures reduce the spatial qualities of an area. Branching characteristics on the tree and shadows on the lawn also provide aesthetic qualities.

Tree Associations

To develop a tree planting concept of complementary and coordinated tree planting, the trees chosen must be grouped into associations. *Tree associations* are a group of trees which are aesthetically harmonious as well as having similar environmental preferences and tolerances. For example, maples and birches or maples and crabapples provide compatible colors and textures; evergreens provide a background for flowering trees; oaks and gums provide similar textures; and ash and elm are also similar in texture. Each association, however, must share a common soil preference, while the tree size and environmental preferences will provide the flexibility necessary to select a tree for a specific location.

Using the lot size as an indication of relative home value and potential area for tree growth, the lists should also be sorted according to mature tree stature, color, and visual effect.

Municipal versus Commercial Nurseries

Municipal nurseries have been around for a long time. In the early part of the twentieth century, many municipalities operated nurseries because it was the only way to have trees available for municipal purposes. During this time, native, wild trees were transplanted to the nursery where they could be pruned and grown until they reached a desirable size for planting on the street. The

Tree shapes. *Top:* Champion Japanese Tree Lilac is an example of an irregular tree shape. *Bottom left:* Norway Maple is rounded (*courtesy Larry Leigh Christian*). *Bottom right:* Champion Normandi Spruce is pyramidal.

Tree shapes. *Top left:* This variety of sugar maple is columnar. *Top right:* Champion White Willow is vase-shaped. *Bottom left:* Weeping Willow is a weeping type. *Bottom right:* Champion Wintergreen Scotch Pine is fastigate.

Flowering crabapples.

trees were often started as seedlings, so the cost was very low. The trees were allowed to grow at their own pace, and when they reached the right size, they were moved to their final site. Municipal nurseries were considered growing areas instead of growth production areas.

Municipal nurseries increased in popularity and number during the 1970s because of federal assistance and labor. As the funding sources decreased in the 1980s, the number of nurseries declined. In 1990, the SMA conducted a survey of its members to get information about municipal nurseries. Of those responding to the

Municipal nursery in Toledo, Ohio.

survey, 71 percent operated a municipal nursery. The cities ranged in size from 30,000 to 400,000 people and averaged 49.7 square miles. The cities had an existing street tree population average of 41,750 trees. Of those cities having a municipal nursery, they had an average of 7682 trees in cultivation, and the trees were planted as seedlings or whips up to 8 feet tall and were grown for an average of 6.5 years. They grew to an average 2.5-inch diameter and increased in value from $3.55 for the whip to $133.00 for the tree. The cities had an average of 75.6 different varieties of trees in their nurseries with the most popular genus or species being Callery Pear, oak, pine, ash, maple, honeylocust, crabapples, and Tulip Tree. Of the stock leaving the nursery, 34 percent was bare-root (BR), 22 percent was balled and burlapped (B&B), and 44 percent was removed by tree spade. Only two of the cities used the tree spade exclusively. There were 1.2 tree spades per nursery, and they were either 30 or 32 inches and 44 inches. The average planting crew was 7.3 people who planted 85 trees each. All the respondents indicated an additional purchase of up to 1000 B&B as well as BR trees from commercial nurseries although the average reflected that fewer BR trees were actually planted. The most commonly planted trees included maples, oaks, ash, honeylocusts, linden, and pears. The most unusual species were Osage Orange, Goldenrain, Water Oak, Hardy Rubber Tree, Bald Cypress, Japanese Tree Lilac, Black Alder, and Pagoda Tree.

There are many positive reasons for operating municipal nurseries just as there are many positive features for purchasing trees from a commercial nursery. The following pros and cons apply to the municipal nursery:

Pros	Cons
Lower cost for the same tree in a commercial nursery.	Lining out stock of new varieties must be purchased.
Native trees grown from seedlings.	Stock does not get maximum care.
Nursery crews can shift from routine maintenance to planting during the season.	Planting season, during extremely busy time of year, puts strain on crew availability.
Nonnursery crews can work in the nursery during bad weather or a slow season.	Must use all trees. Rejects cannot be used or sold.
	No competitive bid on prices.
	Limited selection of varieties.

The best solution to choosing between municipal versus commercial nurseries is to use a combination of the two. This means using the municipal nursery to grow inexpensive, easy-to-grow stock that can be grown more cheaply than in a commercial operation. Use the commercial nursery for the new cultivars, grafted stock, plants that are grown for special locations and plants that are grown more cheaply or are of higher quality than those from the municipal nursery. Municipal nurseries may also be used as hospitals where damaged trees can recover and reshape themselves for several years at little or no cost.

Savings could be even better if municipalities were to sign contracts or letters of agreement with commercial nurseries for trees at a future date. Nurseries can lower prices if they know there will be a guaranteed sale for their products. A variation on this theme is to have the city purchase the lining out stock and send it to a grower who bills the city an annual maintenance fee. The grower also charges the city a digging fee when the trees are planted on the street. This arrangement results in total costs that are 10 to 15 percent less than market prices because of minimal risk to the grower and because the cost is paid as the work is being done rather than at the end. Most municipalities are given wholesale prices from commercial growers; however, occasionally a bid price will be even lower than wholesale. When selecting varieties, municipalities should also take advantage of quantity discounts.

It is imperative that the municipal arborist keep up to date on the latest developments in new varieties of disease- and pest-resistant stock, new trees that will tolerate the local climate through salt tolerance, hardiness, and scorch resistance.

Tree Planting Techniques

Planting a tree represents an investment for the community, and every effort should be made to ensure the greatest chance for a tree's survival. If a municipal street tree dies, the highest percentage of losses occurs during the first growing season after planting. Losses can be avoided through proper handling of the tree followed by care during the first growing season. Trees should be planted at the proper depth, correctively pruned, watered, mulched, and fertilized, as mentioned later in this chapter.

Tree Selection

The performance of trees in the landscape depends on how well the species are suited for the specific site where they are to grow. The tree selection should be based upon the mature size of the tree and whether the site can accommodate the roots for this tree at maturity.

One planting recommendation has remained unchanged over the years: A quality tree is the best investment. Nursery-grown trees are more likely to survive a transplanting than trees dug from the woods. Root systems of nursery-grown trees are compact and are less likely to be injured when they are dug.

Proper planting is one of the critical steps in the life of a tree. Start by selecting the right tree for the right location and soil type. Do not plant sun-loving trees in the shade or shade-loving trees in the sun. Know the soil requirements for the tree. Do not plant tall trees under utility wires, next to buildings, or within 20 feet of other tall trees. If space (400 cubic feet minimum) is not available to accommodate the root system, a tree should not be planted. If the site has poor drainage and it is not possible to correct that, the best alternative is to plant trees that will tolerate saturated soils. These include Red Maple (*Acer rubrum*), Tupelo (*Nyssa sylvatica*), London Plane Tree (*Plantanus acerifolia*), Swamp White Oak (*Quercus bicolor*), Willow Oak (*Quercus phellos*), Bald Cypress (*Taxodium distichum*), and Basswood (*Tilia americana*).

The amount of roots left on the tree is critical to its survival. For bare-root trees, a 2-inch caliper tree should have a minimum root spread of 32 inches. If the tree has a root ball, the ball diameter is 24 inches and its depth is about 16 inches.

Site Selection

Whenever public laws provide the opportunity, street trees should be set behind the sidewalk even if on private property. This allows the trees to be healthier and grow more quickly so the desired street canopy is achieved just as rapidly as with a tree planted in compacted soil beside the street. Furthermore, the setback planting avoids conflict with roots that lift sidewalks, dropping limbs, accidents, car doors, road salt, and automobile fumes which hinder tree growth. Another advantage of this concept is that the municipality has the option of letting the homeowner maintain the tree after planting, which in the long run will reduce the city's maintenance program and costs.

The key to a healthy tree consists of matching the tree to the site and then giving the roots plenty of room to grow. Since the tree's roots will grow as far as there are nutrients, oxygen, and water in noncompacted soil, the more soil available for urban street trees, the better it is for the tree. This means planting trees in a continuous pit or very large raised planters or in groups. Also keep in mind the effects of trees on adjoining land uses when a site is chosen. For example, evergreens that shade the streets and cause icing conditions in colder climates should not be planted, whereas the same evergreens that block winter winds can reduce winter home-heating costs.

There is a tendency to plant young trees close together for an immediate visual impact. Many early street tree planting programs emphasized close spacing, with as little as 20 to 30 feet between trees. These trees became expensive to prune, while mutual shading created deadwood and live branches interfered with each other. Today, spacing standards relate to the mature size of the species planted. For example, trees attaining a small mature size are planted a minimum of 25 feet apart; medium trees, 35 feet; and large trees, 55 feet. Spacing also relates to the width of the tree lawn, since the species selected will be influenced by available growing space for its mature size. In other words, small trees do best in narrow tree lawns while large trees should not be planted in any tree lawn less than 10 feet wide.

Also consider drainage, irrigation, aeration, and underground utilities in selecting tree sites. Many problems can be solved by planting trees in shared root space. This root space contains a large area of proper, uniform soil, and a large number of trees and shrubs can be grown to mature size in a healthier environment.

The planting season varies with the region, plant, and planting method. The experience and advice of established arborists in the region can provide this information. Bare-root trees are best planted when the leaves are off the trees. Spring is best in northern or high-wind regions. B&B trees or trees grown in containers can be planted any time the soil is workable and there is at least 1 month of growing season left for root development before the ground freezes. Trees that form roots slowly in the spring and fall should be planted only in the spring. Trees in this situation include oaks, poplars, Tulip Trees, hornbeams, birches, Goldenrain Trees, evergreens, maples, magnolias, Zelkovas, and sourwoods. Ginkgo and ash generate roots equally fast in spring and fall and can be planted at either time. Linden and yews generate roots more rapidly in the fall, but can be planted in spring or fall.

Blocks versus Mixed Planting

Street tree plantings can be designed in one of two layouts depending upon the city, past practice, and location in the United States.

Block planting means that an entire block of a city street will have only one species of tree planted. Ideally the trees are all planted at the same time. This lowers the maintenance requirements considerably because maintenance should be approximately the same on each tree. Aesthetically, some people feel this approach is better because all trees look identical on the block, which unifies a neighborhood with a common species. The spacing can be equal, and in the midwest and western states, this planting concept is quite compatible with the grid of the street patterns. This design provides a feeling of unity and aesthetic compatibility. The diversification formula is not violated since the next block contains a totally different species. However, this planting style can mean planting trees in inappropriate locations, and a disease or pest could wipe out the whole block at once.

Mixed planting means diversity because each tree on a city block might be totally different from the tree next to it. The trees can all have different spacing, sizes, and shapes. Many cities prefer this design approach because as each house is different, so the trees are also different. This design is customarily found along the east coast and in places where the streets flow in random or curvilinear patterns. With this planting concept the trees tend to be healthier because diseases cannot progress from one tree to the next, root grafts are not likely, and trees grow naturally in random sizes, shapes, spacing, and species. This pattern also allows for a naturalized appearance of the planting, with small trees under the utility wires and large trees over these wires and the mix of plantings side by side. However, maintenance costs will be slightly

Top left and right: Mixed planting and block planting. *Bottom:* Mixed and block planting on each side.

Top: Block plantings on public property with mixed plantings on private land. (*Courtesy Bruce D. Austin.*) *Bottom:* Block plantings make pruning more cost-efficient. Unfortunately, the trees are too big for the site. (*Courtesy Larry Leigh Christian.*)

higher, and there will not be uniformity, if this is important.

On some occasions both planting concepts can be used. As illustrated in the photographs on the previous pages, block planting is used in front of stores and parking lots of a commercial development. The uniformity of the trees provides a visual effect of harmony which signifies that the uses behind the trees are consistently business ventures.

On the other side of the street is a residential area that has a mixed planting. The mix complements each residence as well as the personalities of individuals who live in these homes. The landscape treatment can also be effective in screening and blocking views into and out of the property.

Planting

B&B versus BR versus Container versus Tree Spade

Trees can be purchased in four different ways depending upon the size of the tree and the money available. The form most commonly selected by municipal tree departments is the balled-and-burlapped (B&B) tree. If the root balls are hard and are laced on the sides like an old-fashioned drum, they were dug with the whole root ball intact. However, if the burlap is tied on top or the ball is soft, chances are that the tree was dug bare-root and just stuck into the burlap with some soil. Remember to always remove plastic, brown artificial burlap, and green burlap at planting time. Brown natural burlap, however, can be rolled down and left around the base of the ball, and it should decay in 6 weeks underground.

The second most common form of transplanting is bare-root (BR). Trees up to 3 inches in diameter may be planted with bare roots. Bare-root trees may have more roots than B&B trees but have fewer surviving root hairs, needed to ensure planting success. BR trees can easily be given hormones to promote root regeneration. These hormones are available as sprays, dips, or soaks. BR trees are also dug while the tree is dormant, and they may be kept in cold storage overwinter. Care must be taken to prevent them from drying out, to keep them dormant, and to keep the temperature below 45°F prior to planting. BR trees must be planted as soon as possible after delivery to ensure a high survival rate. If planting is not possible, they should be healed in or kept dormant, cool, and moist.

Container-grown trees are excellent for small to medium stock. Containerized trees can be planted during most of the year. Care should be taken in planting containerized trees to be sure that the

Top: Planting a B&B Summit Ash. *Bottom:* Custom planting truck owned by the forestry department.

roots have not circled the container. Roots that have circled the container should be loosened, cut, and removed. Some periphery roots can also be extended out and into the backfill to encourage rapid plant establishment and sturdier trees.

The tree spade saves a lot of labor and allows fairly large trees to be moved almost any time during the growing season. Be sure that the tree is not too large for the spade size and that not too many roots are cut by the blades. The spade can also glaze the soil, especially if it has a high clay content. Glazing retards root penetration from the root ball into the surrounding soil, but this problem can be corrected by roughening the sides of the hole prior to planting.

Hole and Soil Preparation

According to the latest research, reported by American Forests, trees do best if planted in a large planting area that is wide but not deep, where the soil is loose and suited for root growth. The planting area should be 5 times the diameter of the planting ball. A rototiller or shovel should be used to loosen and mix the soil in the entire area to a depth of about 12 inches. Organic matter can be added to the loosened soil as long as the new material is mixed uniformly throughout the area. In the center of the prepared area, dig a shallow hole to set the tree. The hole should allow the root ball to sit on solid ground rather than in loose soil. Once the ball is set in the hole, its upper surface should be level with the existing soil. Experiments have shown that root growth in plain soil is no different from or better than in a soil with amendments such as peat, perlite, or sawdust. If the planting soil is all rubble or requires drainage, new soil should be brought in and the drainage corrected. Excessive peat moss in the planting hole will act as a sponge and cause the tree to drown. It also encourages a fibrous root ball that does not extend into the surrounding soil. This results in high stress to the tree during droughts and causes it to have a short life span. If a soil must be created, an ideal soil system should have the following: air, 25 percent; water, 25 percent; organic matter, 5 percent; minerals, 45 percent. Plants need the following for good growth:

Water

Permeability

Aeration

Fertility

Soil density

Drainage

Maintenance

In situations, such as tree lawns or sidewalks, where a tree must be planted but space will not allow planting in a manner suggested above, other techniques must be used. The planting hole should have an enlarged top, and the soil should be replaced with loosened parent material if the soil is good or improved soil when the soil is very poor. Drainage is vital to the tree's survival and must be correct at planting time. The hole must be wide enough to accommodate the ball and roots without bending any roots. If necessary, improve the soil for root space under the adjacent sidewalk. According to a wise old saying, "You should plant a 50-cent tree in a $5 hole."

Planting

Once the site is prepared, the tree is set in the hole. It should be removed from its container, and all rope, wire, and artificial burlap should be removed from the ball. Natural burlap should be loosened, rolled back from the top, and slit along the sides. Position the tree so that it is vertical and its branches will not cause harm to street traffic, pedestrians, or an abutter. Once the tree is set in the hole, the soil should be added gradually. For bare-root trees, work the soil firmly at the base of the roots. Then add more soil and work it under and around the lower roots. The tree may be raised and lowered gently during the filling process to eliminate air pockets and to bring the roots in close contact with the soil. When the roots are just covered, add water, let the soil settle, and finish filling the hole with loose soil. The planting of a B&B or containerized tree follows the same concept except that the backfill soil is lightly packed around the root ball. Water will settle the soil and remove air pockets better than packing with feet. After the filling is completed, rake a 4-inch dike to form a saucer around the circumference at the planting hole. The saucer will catch water and prevent runoff for a short time after planting. The ground should be leveled off before winter sets in, since the water may freeze and injure the trunk and may also encourage the root growth to remain within the berm close to the tree. It is better to keep the soil loose to accept watering than to make a saucer that will last over winter. Also be sure the tree is 1 inch higher than it grew in the nursery.

The secret to successful planting is keeping the roots out of the ground for the shortest possible time. It has been said that for every

30 seconds a root hair is exposed to wind and sun, the survival rate is cut by 50 percent.

Pruning

When a tree is being transplanted, only 4 or 5 percent of the tree's roots are taken with the tree. However, pruning one-third of the treetop to compensate for the root loss is not necessary. It is better to keep the roots well watered and growing than to remove the leaves and food source for the tree. Root replacement can take up to 5 years on a 4-inch tree; on a proportionately larger 10-inch tree, 12 years is needed to restore root development. Therefore, transplant large trees for immediate effect and design purposes only. For tree vigor, smaller is better.

When you are doing the actual planting, check over the tree to remove all dead, broken, damaged, or weak branches as well as roots. All kinked and girdling roots should be cut as well as all roots growing around on the inside of a container-grown tree. Don't hesitate to reject a tree with severe root problems. When pruning the top of the tree, determine the desired shape of the tree, prune to correct structural weakness, and start proper pruning 1 or 2 years after planting.

Watering

Water is very critical to a newly planted tree. Since one factor always limits growth and because only 5 percent of the roots are there, water absorption is limited. The hole should be filled with water when the planting is halfway done and when the tree is completely planted. Water does the best job of settling the soil around the tree's roots. The saucer should again be filled with water, twice within 24 hours after planting. After the original planting, a thorough watering that soaks in once a week is sufficient if less than 1 inch of rain has fallen. On extremely hot or windy days, a very fine misting of the leaves may be necessary, several times a day. This process cools the leaves and slows water loss from inside the tree. Watering may also be necessary during drought periods for a few years after planting. The broad, shallow saucer should be considered temporary, and it should be removed before the first winter.

Fertilizing

Since only 5 percent of the tree's roots are available to absorb fertilizer, it is wasted on newly planted trees. Once the leaves have matured, a light fertilizing can be done. Too much high-nitrogen fertilizer will push leaf development more quickly than the roots can support it. Some researchers feel a high-phosphorus "starter" fertilizer will help root development on newly planted trees. A pH of 6.5 to 7.0 is also desirable for maximum root development. Once the trees are established, a slow-release 10-10-10 or 20-20-20 fertilizer plus 2 to 4 inches of mulch will encourage rapid tree vigor. Slow-release fertilizer packets can be used since the tree will only be able to use the fertilizer once the roots have grown toward it.

Wrapping, Guying, and Staking

The latest research indicates that trees do not need to be wrapped. Wrapping slows the tree's ability to adapt to a new site. A wrapping tape also provides habitat for insects, and the string holding the tape can girdle the tree. If trunk protection is desired, the new tree shelter or plastic, translucent growing tubes are better than tape because they allow sunlight and air to flow around the bark.

Trees should not be staked. If wind is a problem or the tree develops a lean, it can be supported with a flexible stake or guy wire that will permit the tree trunk to sway in the wind. Trunk movement is necessary for building trunk strength. All stakes and guy wire should be removed between 12 and 18 months after planting. For trees up to 20 feet in height, tree stakes are sufficient for support. Larger trees should be guyed. In staking or guying, the first wire should be applied to hold the tree against wind or lean, and the other one or two stakes or guys are placed equally and loosely around the tree. Tree-bracing collars made of flexible plastic or nylon tape, manufactured for this purpose, or twist braces that allow for flexibility of the tree trunk should be used instead of hose and wire. These braces are also recyclable. The exception to this use of hose and wire is indicated later for low-maintenance planting.

Mulch

Mulch should be spread around newly planted trees. The mulch can be bark, wood chips, pine needles, corn cobs, sawdust, or any other locally available product that will simulate the natural conditions of the forest floor. Plastic mulch or plastic under mulch is not recommended. The mulch should let moisture and air enter the soil. It should also eliminate the competition from weeds and grass while providing organic matter to the soil as it decomposes. Most importantly, keep mowers and string trimmers away from the tree trunk. The mulch should be spread only 2 to 4 inches deep because more than 4 inches will smother the tree roots, although current research may be disproving this long-held notion. The mulch decomposition rate should be checked annually and new mulch added if necessary.

Planting Out of Season

If a tree must be dug in full-leaf, the tree should be root-pruned at the nursery prior to digging. The tree should be hand dug so the root ball is balled and burlapped in the hole. After digging, the root ball must be soaked and kept in a shady misting area for 3 to 7 days until the new growth has hardened off. After the tree is dug, up to one-third of the leaves should be removed and antidessicant sprayed on the foliage. The tree should be planted as soon as possible after it leaves the misting area. It is also critical that the tree be watered immediately after planting. Then it should be watered at least twice a week for the rest of the growing season.

Low-Maintenance Planting

What happens when a project actually receives little or no maintenance after the landscape contractor has left the site and no one removes the guy wires? Many times on interstate highways, large parklands, and other projects in which large numbers of trees have been planted, the guying systems are left on the trees for many, many years. This results in girdled and deformed trees, sometimes dead trees, and in almost every case trees that are not as healthy as they should be. To correct this problem where low maintenance is anticipated, arborists should consider a biodegradable guy system which will provide the necessary guidance during the first 2 years; then the system can fall apart, leaving the tree to grow unimpeded.

The specifications should state that the trees must be as healthy as possible, vigorous, well-rooted, and representative of the species. A certificate should be required to guarantee that the tree was nursery-grown and grew within a 200-mile radius of the project site. The certificate should also include the date of the last transplanting and the age and grade of the tree.

Pruning of new trees should be minimized and done by people skilled in this work. The pruning should remove only the dead, diseased, damaged, or crossing branches. All pruning should be done in accordance with accepted nursery and horticultural practices.

As is often the case in large planting projects, the contractor is given the option of planting trees and shrubs with either balled and burlapped or container-grown plant material. In either case, the planting hole should adhere to the principles stated earlier in this chapter. The planting depth should vary so that the tree will be planted within 1 inch of the depth to which it was grown in the nursery. If the tree is balled and burlapped, the burlap and the rope should be cut or untied from the ball prior to backfilling and at least one-third of the burlap and all the wire and rope should be removed. If the burlap is treated or not biodegradable, it should be completely removed. If the tree is container-grown, it should have been grown in the container for at least 1 year prior to this planting. All containers should be removed from the tree or shrub.

The guy wires chosen for these low-maintenance trees should be 18-gauge uncoated steel wire. The contractor should not coat the wire or retard the rusting process. Contractors can obtain this wire directly from wire manufacturers. While 18-gauge wire may seem thin, it has been calculated to withstand 95-mile-per-hour winds blowing against an evergreen tree with a 14-foot-high wind sail. The important thing to remember is that the guy wires should be secured by twisting the wires around themselves and should be equally spaced around the tree, with one guy wire installed in the direction of the prevailing wind. The turnbuckle can be typical for the industry provided it has a 4-inch lengthwise opening fitted with eye screws and located halfway between the tree and the stake. The turnbuckle with rusted wire on either side will eventually fall to the ground and rust away over a period of years. Where flagging is required, white rags should be tied to the guy wires at the turnbuckle. These rags will also deteriorate in about 2 years. The wire should be anchored to the ground with softwood stakes which are 2×2×30 inches, unpainted and driven at an angle to a depth of at least 15 inches. Any excess length can be cut off at the ground level. By selecting softwood stakes, they will eventually rot into the soil and within 5 years completely disappear from around the tree.

The protective hose should be cut from a rubber hose and not a nylon or plastic hose. The minimum size should be about $\frac{3}{4}$-inch diameter and 8 inches long. The hose should deteriorate within 2 to 3 years, while the wire is rusting and breaking, and not cause the tree any harm. The deterioration should occur when the need for guying no longer exists. The wire in the hose can be secured between the first and second branches or at two-thirds the tree height, which is standard in the industry.

The backfill mixture for trees planted under this specification should follow the information presented earlier. During the backfilling process, two fertilizer packets or pellets should be

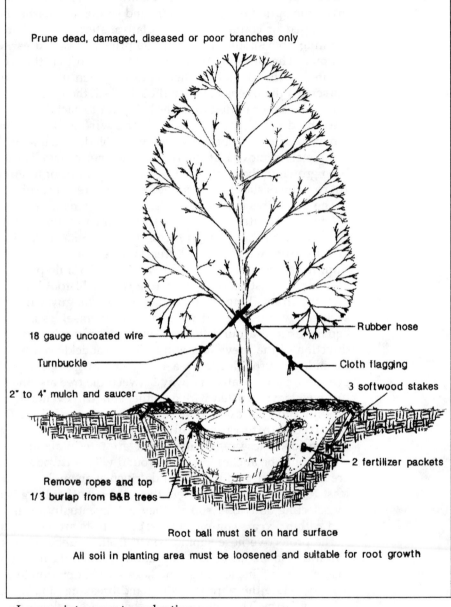

Prune dead, damaged, diseased or poor branches only

18 gauge uncoated wire

Turnbuckle

2" to 4" mulch and saucer

Remove ropes and top
1/3 burlap from B&B trees

Rubber hose

Cloth flagging

3 softwood stakes

2 fertilizer packets

Root ball must sit on hard surface

All soil in planting area must be loosened and suitable for root growth

Low-maintenance tree planting.

placed 8 to 10 inches deep on either side of the ball. The packets should contain 16-8-16 fertilizer which is certified by the manufacturer to provide controlled release for a minimum of 6 years. After the tree is in place, the backfilling is finished and the soil is firmed by water to eliminate all air pockets.

After the tree has been planted and the guy wires have been installed, the turnbuckles should be tightened to keep the tree upright against the prevailing wind. The other turnbuckles are loose. These turnbuckles should be checked at least twice during the period of the contract to ensure that the tree remains upright. Also during the planting process, a 4-inch-high mound should be formed around the tree to make a saucer. The saucer must be flooded with water at least 3 times within the first 24 hours after the tree has been planted. Thereafter the tree should be watered thoroughly at least once a week for the period of the contract or one growing season, whichever is longer. A 4-inch layer of wood chips or other suitable organic mulch should be applied between the first two waterings.

In projects where this low-maintenance tree planting technique has been applied, it has been found that the trees have survived with a typical 90 to 95 percent success rate. Two and three years after planting, all traces of the guying system have broken from the tree, the trees have remained upright, and the trees are growing at a rapid rate. This approach was compared by the author to another project where the standard specifications were applied 12 years earlier. The guy wires were still on many of the trees, and the trees were girdled, were dead, had secondary leader development, or had the cable and hose ingrown to the tree. The lack of fertilizer and water saucer also contributed to less than a 40 percent success rate.

So many times a contractor plants the tree and leaves it for someone else to maintain. When a lack of communication or a lack of funds prevents follow-through in the tree's care, only the trees suffer. Later the landscape declines, and the owner gets the blame and must take the responsibility to correct the damage.

Follow-up

Newly planted trees will require special care for 2 or 3 years. Large trees will need this care for 5 to 10 years. This care includes watering during droughts; light fertilization; pruning for proper shape and removal of undesirable, dead, or diseased branches; mulch reapplication; and anything else an onsite inspection might indicate.

Grass should always be kept away from the base of the tree, and flowers can be planted at the base after the tree has become established. Also avoid application of herbicides anywhere in the vicinity of newly planted trees. Preemergent herbicides can be used with extreme caution and attention to the manufacturer's instructions and the label's requirements.

If a tree should die, care should be taken to determine the cause before another tree is planted. If poor drainage is a problem, it should be corrected. If vandalism is a problem, have neighborhood kids help plant larger trees in these areas. The kids will develop a sense of "ownership" which will help protect the tree from vandalism. Also add a large stake, 5 feet tall, beside a tree to help protect it for its first 2 years. Plant smaller trees in the parks and residential areas where vandalism is less likely to be a problem. If vandalism still occurs, consider the reasons for vandalism and make the necessary corrections before replanting. Typical reasons for vandalism include planting at the wrong site, planting without "their" permission or input, planting the wrong size or species, planting in a rival gang's "turf," etc.

In areas of high pedestrian traffic, it may be necessary to install pavers—stone or brick—set in sand over the tree ball. This will have a negative impact on the tree's growth. In areas where all else fails, a tree container can be used. The container should be obtained commercially to ensure a high-strength, engineered pot. It is also best that the container be insulated on the sides and have an irrigation system or water reservoir built in. The best containers have fill pipes, overflow-drains, and reservoir drains. Containerized trees require weekly watering and constant attention.

With proper planting and maintenance, the millions of new trees that will be planted in the 1990s will survive and be an asset to the planet.

Sources

ACRT: *Vancouver Street Tree Plan*, Kent, OH, 1990.

Boener, Deborah A.: "Nurturing New Trees," *Urban Forests*, July/August 1990, p. 6.

Bassuk, Nina, and Pat Lindsey: "The Urban Jungle," *Grounds Maintenance*, June 1991, p. 11.

Baumgardt, Dr. John P.: "GM Guide to Planting a Tree," *Grounds Maintenance*, Oct. 1975, p. 38.

Cinque, Marie T.: "Precautions for Digging and Transplanting out of Season," *Weeds, Trees and Turf*, August 1979, p. 46.

Despres, Ronald E.: "Suburban Street Tree Planting," *Public Works*, July 1982, p. 56.

Foster, Ruth S.: "Planting a Better Tree," *Boston Globe*, April 14, 1991, p. 14 North.

Harris, Dr. Richard W.: "Early Care of Trees in the Landscape," *American Nurseryman*, September 15, 1976, p. 14.

Containerized planting.

Miller, Dr. Robert W.: *Urban Forestry, Planning and Managing Urban Greenspaces,* Prentice-Hall, Englewood Cliffs, NJ, 1988.

Moll, Gary A.: "The Best Way to Plant Trees," *Urban Forests,* March/April 1990, p. 8.

Patterson, Dr. James C.: "Soil and Design Considerations," *City Trees,* January/February 1991, p. 12.

Phillips, Leonard E., Jr.: "Solution to the Greenhouse Effect," *City Trees,* January/February 1989, p. 4.

Phillips, Leonard E., Jr.: "Low Maintenance Tree Planting Specifications," *City Trees,* March 1986, p. 12.

Phillips, Leonard E., Jr.: "Tree Bracing Collars," *City Trees,* April 1986, p. 6.

Phillips, Leonard E., Jr.: *Municipal Street Tree Master Planning,* Peabody, MA, 1981.

Pirone, P. P., Hartman, J. R., Sall, M. A., and Pirone, T. P.: *Tree Maintenance,* 6th ed., Oxford University Press, New York, 1988.

"Researching Maintenance," *Grounds Maintenance,* August 1991, p. 1.

"Results of Reader's Survey—Municipal Tree Nursery," *City Trees,* May/June 1991, p. 10.

Shigo, Alex L.: *A New Tree Biology*, Shigo and Trees, Assoc.,
Durham, NH, 1989.
Watson, Dr. Gary: "Disorders Caused by Root Related Stresses,"
City Trees, September/October 1990, p. 15.
Whitcomb, Carl E.: "Factors Affecting the Establishment of Urban
Trees," *Journal of Arboriculture*, 5(10): 217–219, October 1979.

Endnote

Special thanks to the following nurseries for information in their catalogs and correspondence to *City Trees:* Bobtown; Carlisle; Flax Mill; Green Leaf; Lake County; Princeton; Schichtel's; J. Frank Schmidt; Siebenthaler; J. Verkade; Wayside; Weston; and Willis. Special thanks for technical assistance to Greg Kane (Lake County Nursery).

5
Tree Care

Tree Pruning

Trees are pruned to preserve their health and appearance while keeping them safe for people and property. Pruning also enhances the structural integrity, longevity, and functional value of trees in the urban environment. Trees must be pruned to remove dead, damaged, and dangerous limbs. Pruning can be performed at any time of the year except bud break. Timing, such as immediately after flowering and not during heavy sap flow, is also critical to certain species. Pruning should be performed only by workers who have been trained in proper arboricultural techniques. To the untrained eye, a tree may appear to be in good condition, but the trained arborist with years of experience can spot problems and defects long before they become hazardous. Before any work is done, the tree should be inspected for hazards such as leaning trunks, broken limbs, split crotches, visible root problems, diseases, and dead wood. All hazards should be reported to the supervisor, owner, and tree worker.

Pruning Young Trees

Pruning young trees consists primarily of training young trees to develop proper shapes and structural strength, to remove any dead or damaged branches, and to have low maintenance at maturity. Young street trees should be pruned to ensure a straight, strong trunk; one central leader; high branches; and a well-balanced crown. Three years after planting, young trees should be pruned to remove any dead, damaged, diseased, or objectional branches. Five years after planting, trees should receive a class I pruning, defined below.

Pruning of young branches directs the growth according to the direction of the buds (see sketch A). Pruning also encourages vigor in the remaining branches. Small wounds heal fast. Although it is

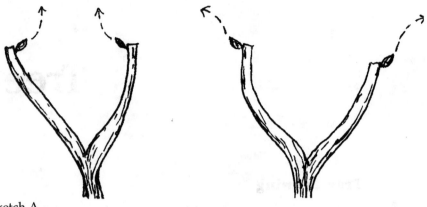

Sketch A.

not always possible, the best time to prune is when the trees are dormant.

Maintenance Pruning

Pruning of mature trees falls into one of four classes. The 1988 revised *Pruning Standards for Shade Trees,* written by the National Arborist Association,* can be summarized as follows:

Class I, fine pruning   Fine pruning shall consist of the removal of dead, diseased, damaged, objectionable, and weak branches on the main trunks and limbs which are larger than ½ inch in diameter. (This procedure requires the most time and greatest skill per tree, and most municipalities cannot afford the expense of class I pruning on street trees.)

Class II, standard pruning   Standard pruning shall consist of the removal of dead, diseased, damaged, objectionable, and weak branches which are larger than 1 inch in diameter.

Class III, hazard pruning   Hazard pruning shall consist of the removal of the dead, diseased, and damaged branches larger than 2 inches in diameter.

Class IV, crown reduction pruning   Crown reduction, cutting back, or drop-crotching consists of the reduction of tops, sides, or individual limbs. This procedure is used near utility lines, at significant crown dieback, to correct storm damage or for topiary reasons. (This procedure is generally not recommended for municipal street trees.)

*These standards have been rewritten slightly in 1992 as part of ANSI A.300.

Heritage Trees

Some communities designate certain trees as desirable because of their age, historical significance, aesthetic or horticultural value, visibility, size, etc. Extra efforts are made to keep these trees healthy, vigorous, and protected while nonheritage trees are left alone, receive little maintenance, and are removed when they are close to death. Heritage trees are kept alive long after their useful life because of their importance.

Pruning Techniques

The methods used in pruning and branch removal will vary depending upon the size, species, and function of the plant. Street trees are best pruned according to the following guidelines, summarized again from *Pruning Standards for Shade Trees:*

1. All cuts should be made as close as possible to the trunk or parent limb, without cutting into the branch collar or leaving a protruding stub (see sketch B). For small branches being cut at a bud, avoid a steep angle of cut and being too far from or too close to the bud (see sketch C).
2. All branches too large to support with one hand should be precut to avoid splitting or tearing of the bark. To precut is to remove the branch safely by first undercutting, then overcutting 3 or 4 inches from the crotch. The third cut removes the stub (see sketch D). When you are shortening a branch, the lateral branch should be at least one-half the diameter of the branch being removed so weak sprouts are not forced to grow (see sketch E).
3. Treatment of cuts with wound dressing is not recommended.
4. Old injuries, cables, and screw rods should be inspected.
5. Sharp tools that make clean cuts should be used at all times.
6. All cut limbs should be removed from the tree. Small branches can be thrown clear of lower branches and obstructions. Larger branches must be lowered with ropes.
7. Pruning should be timed so as to avoid insect or disease infestation.
8. Remove the weaker or less desirable crossed branches.
9. No more than one-third of the total leaf area should be pruned at one time, unless sucker growth is desired.
10. Visible girdling roots should be cut at either end and removed.

Sketch B.

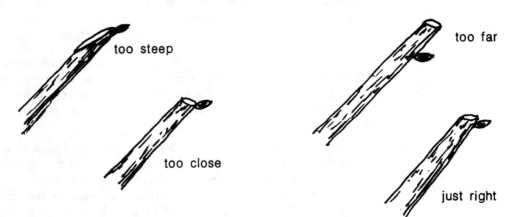

Sketch C.

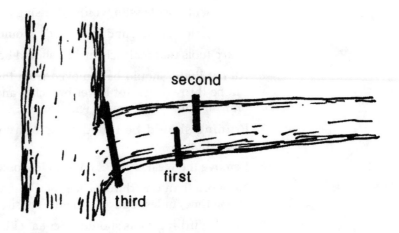

Sketch D.

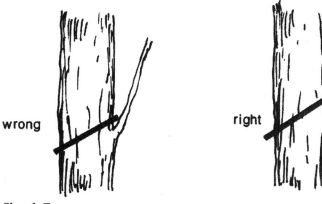

wrong

right

Sketch E.

When branches are properly removed, the callus will grow equally around the entire cut, forming a ring or doughnut. The proper cut at the collar heals much more quickly than the flush cut. Climbing irons should not be used on live trees except for tree removal or emergency rescue. Keep in mind that whenever a gaffe enters the tree or a branch is cut, the tree is injured. This allows decay-causing microorganisms, diseases, and insects to enter the tree before it can compartmentalize and a callus can cover the wound.

Utility Pruning

Street trees that interfere with electric distribution lines must be pruned back a prescribed distance depending upon the line voltage. This pruning is usually done by contractors of the electric utility. In some cities the contractor is the city's tree department. In other cities, the municipal tree departments are prevented from pruning near the wires due to liability. All tree workers should be trained in how to work safely around wires. They should also be familiar with the safety requirements of ANSI's Z133.1-1988 and the A-300 pruning standards, released in 1992.

In some locations, trimming around electric wires is a class IV pruning technique where large branches are cut back and the treetop nearest the wires is reduced. Large entire branches should be removed at laterals, and all remaining branches should be directed away from the wires. Try to keep the natural shape of the tree as much as possible.

Fortunately, class II is more common, although some trees are pruned to allow the lines to pass through the tree. Cuts should be made at crotches to encourage growth away from the lines. Efforts must be made to prevent sprouting. This is accomplished by making cuts close to the main stem and clean cuts outside the branch collar and by avoiding excessive wounding.

Pruning Program

Municipalities should first determine which class of pruning they wish to adopt and then set aside funds to meet this goal. Then they should schedule all pruning to occur on a planned rotation or scheduled pruning cycle. A scheduled routine pruning, if on a 3- to 8-year cycle, should minimize the need for demand pruning. Demand pruning involves sending crews all over the city to answer service requests from the public and political leaders. Costs for demand pruning are usually twice the cost per tree of scheduled pruning. Cities that keep pruning on a planned rotation program have high worker productivity because of efficient work scheduling and reduced travel time, since several trees might be pruned at a single setup. This program also reduces the number of complaints from overpruning because the most growth that might be removed is 3 to 8 years' worth. Since the branches being removed are smaller with scheduled pruning, the wound size is smaller and the tree's recovery, callus formation, and subsequent vigor are all quickly restored. There will also be fewer emergencies, dead limbs, and demand calls on frequently pruned trees. Storm damage is likely to be less on vigorous, well pruned trees. Healthier trees eliminate the need for spraying, cabling, and bracing. Trees that are in excellent condition will rate higher in the appraisal formula. Healthier trees also look better and provide an enhanced aesthetic value to the community.

Once a routine pruning cycle is established and a couple of cycles have been completed, certain trees will reach a point where pruning is not necessary. The cycle should be continued, however, because all trees can benefit from the inspection regardless of whether pruning is done, and certain other trees will always need pruning. Because systematic pruning improves tree health, IPM programs are needed less often, there is less potential for damage claims against the city, and removal costs are deferred because the trees live longer. A tree climber and aerial lift can handle 40 miles of street tree pruning plus 500 park trees a year on a routine schedule. This is twice the rate of demand pruning.

Performance Standards

The rates at which a tree crew can accomplish various maintenance tasks depend upon the crew and equipment available. Performance standards should be set by determining an average hourly measure over a 4-month period. This is especially easy if the work crew completes a detailed daily work report. This report should indicate the tree size, work to be done, and time on the job. A blank form used in Toledo, Ohio, follows on the next page. Once all this information is tabulated, standards can be completed. Once the standards are completed, they can be used every month to measure the production rate against the standard. A couple of municipal performance standards are illustrated in Table 5-1. As this table clearly illustrates, comparing standards between cities is not always valid because of the wide range of labor, equipment, growth rates, and work standards for each city. It is best that the standards be developed for each individual city based upon its own standards and using Table 5-1 as a guide.

Tree Species

Recent studies indicate that frequently planted trees will vary in pruning needs, based completely on species. The following list indicates pruning needs, by species, in increasing order:

London Plane seldom requires pruning or premature removal. While it does tolerate heavily polluted air, it is sensitive to cold temperature.

Honeylocust tolerates air pollution, drought, and a wide range of soils. This species seldom needs pruning.

Red Maple is weak-wooded and easily damaged by storms but will tolerate heavy soil. Its pruning and removal costs, however, are lower than the average cost to maintain street trees.

White and Red Oak are difficult to transplant, but once established, they seldom need pruning until maturity. At maturity, the tree begins to die slowly, and removal of dead limbs can require 20 years of pruning.

Sugar Maple is not tolerant of the urban environment and requires extensive pruning at maturity. Sugar Maple is intolerant to drought and road salt.

Silver Maple is a fast grower, is weak-wooded, and requires extensive pruning after storms.

Daily Work Report
Division of Parks and Forestry

Date: ___

CREWLEADER SIGNATURE

SUPERVISOR SIGNATURE

Crew Members	Time	
	Reg	O.T.
Crewleader: ___		
Crew: ___		

Equipment	
Trucks:	Saws:

Break Time	Start	Finish
A.M.		
Lunch		
Mileage		
P.M.		

* Work Code Explanation:

1 Street Trim
2 Park Trim
3 Alley Trim
4 Street Removal
5 Park Removal
6 Alley Removal
7 Stump Removal
8 Pick-Ups
9 Hangers
10 Woodlot
11 Storm Dmg. Reg.
12 Storm Dmg. OT
13 Snow Reg.
14 Snow OT
15 Tree Planting
16 Nursery Maintenance
17 Elmdale Time (Cleanup Inventory?)

Special Projects

18 Banners
19 Wood Delivery
20 Brush Removal
21 Painting/Street Light Removal
22 Equipment Downtime (Breakdowns)
23 Downtime
24 Equipment Pickup
25 Meetings
26 Training
27 Benches
28 Newplant Maint.
29 Planting Preparation

Ass. #	Serial Number / Assignment Description	Work Code *	Assignment Time		Clock Hours	Crew Hours	Mileage Arrive	Travel Time	Totals
			Arrive	Depart					
	ELMDALE								
1									
2									
3									
4									
	Page 1 Total								

Pin Oak requires routine pruning of lower branches because of its naturally drooping branch habit. Chlorosis in alkaline soils can cause premature health problems.

Norway Maple requires root pruning when it is planted close to sidewalks, and the lower branches need constant pruning. However, it is also the most frequently planted tree in the United States. Its pruning costs are slightly above the average cost of all tree species listed here. Careful selections of cultivars could reduce the problems with this tree.

American Elm despite its susceptibility to Dutch Elm disease and subsequent removal resulting from the disease, also has weak crotches and wood that is susceptible to storm damage.

Boxelder, Siberian Elm, Willow, and Poplar are not recommended as street trees. Their lifespan is short, they break apart easily in storms, and they are susceptible to several insects and disease attacks. Pruning and removal costs on these trees are the highest of all the tree species compared.

Root Pruning

If roots become exposed and damaged during transplanting, storms, or construction, like branches, they should be pruned. The pruning techniques for roots are identical to those for branches. The cuts should be clean and smooth and at a crotch. Exposed roots should be kept moist, protected from wind and sun, and replanted as quickly as possible.

Emergency Removals

During storms when the priority is to restore street accessibility and electric service, proper pruning will cause unnecessary delays. When emergencies occur, the forestry department must keep records of the calls. Then when the emergency is over, it must return to all the damaged trees and make proper cuts.

Tree Removals

Most cities can plan, through natural attrition, to remove approximately 1 to 2 percent of their tree population every year. A 1 percent removal rate indicates a 100-year lifecycle. Trees have to be removed because of death, endangering or hazardous conditions, untreelike conditions (old, severely pruned trees), and their

Table 5-1. Work Performance Standards

Pruning	Vancouver work hours	Toledo work hours
Young tree	0.33	
Systematic—small to medium trees in bucket	1.6	
Manual	2.0	
Large trees	3.2	
Extra-large trees	3.6	
Tree size: 0–6 inches		0.84
6–12 inches		1.41
12–18 inches		2.29
18–24 inches		3.41
24–30 inches		3.89
30–36 inches		4.43
36–42 inches		4.94
Planting		
Per tree	5.0	
Watering	0.3	
Removal, inches dbh		
0–6	2.1	0.72
6–12	2.8	1.99
12–18	5.2	4.24
18–24	8.9	5.81
24 +	15.3	
24–30		10.58
30–36		14.31
36–42		15.75
Stump removal, inches		
0–6	0.9	1.06
6–12	1.8	1.06
12–18	3.4	1.06

Table 5-1. Work Performance Standards (Continued)

Pruning	Vancouver work hours	Toledo work hours
	Stump removal, inches	
18–24	5.8	1.45
24 +	10.2	
24–30		1.92
30–36		3.03
36–42		3.94

undesirability due to species, poor fruiting habits, or insect or disease problems. Since trees become an emotional issue, the public needs to be educated about this statistic of natural tree loss. If trees are removed before they are dead, their removal can have negative effects. Harvesting trees of a certain age or diameter is generally unacceptable in our society, which is stressing the importance of trees in keeping our planet green. This gives the arborist no choice but to leave trees on their own and prune for safety. When the tree has declined to 90 percent and a new tree is planted, most people are ready to let the old one go.

Root Problems

Tree roots are a major component of every tree. The root hairs grow and become hard and send out new, white, absorbing roots and root hairs. Roots grow laterally as well as at the tips, similar to the way a branch grows. Roots grow well where conditions are adequate. Roots need water, oxygen, and nutrients which are most often supplied near the surface of the soil. Roots do not grow well, if at all, under pavement unless water, oxygen, and nutrients are suitable for adequate growth. More than 50 percent of the active feeding roots are beyond the drip line of the tree. In fact, the roots will usually spread out a distance equal to the height of the tree.

Many tree roots, especially on Norway Maples and willows, will eventually grow right out of the ground. This does not hurt the tree because the feeder roots are still below the surface. This growing out of the ground is actually the diameter expansion on the lateral or structural roots. Since the solid earth below the root cannot readily accept the diameter expansion, most of these roots expand

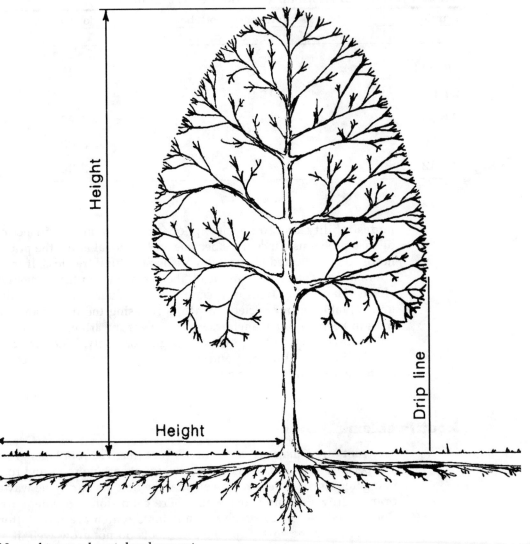

Height

Height

Drip line

Normal tree and root development.

on their top sides, where there is less resistance to growth.

Problems with tree roots begin when shallow-rooted trees are forced to grow in the tree lawn and next to the sidewalk. As the roots increase in diameter, they raise the sidewalks, just as they raise the soil in areas where there is no sidewalk.

When the municipality decides it is time to correct the problems associated with heaved sidewalks and curbs, due to tree roots, a whole series of new problems with the trees can result. Since many of the horizontal roots that are causing the problems are the same roots that make a tree stable against storms and wind, it is not advisable to prune these roots in the interest of saving the walk.

The list below indicates some alternatives developed to deal with sidewalk problems.

1. Remove and replace the trees.
2. Remove and replace the sidewalks, making them higher than before.
3. Work with the engineers and construction managers to understand the problems and reach an agreeable compromise.
4. Use expansion curbing to go around the tree's flare.
5. Use curved sidewalks to avoid trees.
6. Use ramps and elevated sidewalks.
7. Plant trees on private property and at least 4 feet away from the sidewalk, if possible.
8. Use easements to run the sidewalk on private property.
9. Use physical root barriers, but do *not* cut major roots to install the barrier.
10. Chemically treat the asphalt and concrete walks to retard root invasion.
11. Install a biobarrier by Typar, which is a fabric root barrier that is commercially available.
12. Improve soil conditions to help tree roots grow more deeply and minimize sidewalk damage.
13. Have solutions built into construction specifications and subdivision regulations.
14. Remember that the best solutions are long-term ones that involve planting the right tree in the right place.

There is no substitute for careful planning and cooperation with other city officials.

Biobarriers are a popular commercial solution to this problem. Biobarriers come in three types: diversion barriers which form a wall, pervious barriers which allow moisture to penetrate, and chemical barriers which kill root hairs and prevent root development near a chemically treated fabric. A controlled-release chemical treatment works best because the proper dosage is released over a long period. A single application is too strong when installed and is depleted over time. The chemical biobarrier is a

Typar fabric made by Dupont with chemicals impregnated in the fabric. The chemical is released as a gas which, over time, kills growing root hairs. The chemical biobarrier can be applied vertically, horizontally, or around the perimeter of the planting pit.

Sometimes, when no other alternatives can be used, a common solution—but not the best—is to cut the roots, remove them, and then reinstall a sidewalk. When this is done, the crown of the tree should be reduced to cut back on the wind sail and to reduce the liability if the tree should blow over. If the tree cannot be root-pruned and crown-reduced to make it safe, it should be removed.

If more than 50 percent of the tree roots have to be removed, the tree should be removed as well. If 30 percent of the roots have to be removed from one side, the tree should be removed. If the trunk of the tree is 12 inches in diameter or less and soil excavation or root cutting is closer than 3 feet from the trunk, or if the trunk is larger than 12 inches in diameter and the roots have to be cut closer than 6 feet from the trunk, then tree removal should be considered. If any root larger than 2 inches in diameter is cut or removed from one side of the tree, the crown should be reduced on the same side. If time is not a factor, the root pruning should not be done for 1 month on either side of bud break in the spring. All trees with pruned roots should be indicated on the inventory so that annual inspections can be made to check the tree stability and recovery rate. All root pruning should be done by the tree trimming crew in a manner similar to pruning branches.

Tree Maintenance Tips

Once a tree is in the ground, routine maintenance is necessary. This maintenance consists of pruning, watering, disease and pest control, and eventually disposal of the tree. The following are some tips regarding maintenance of trees.

Design and Planting

The best innovative ideas come from careful planning. When one is dealing with trees, planting the right tree in the right place is an adage repeated often. Plant hardy trees that withstand storms and the local environment. Plant trees which fit the site and soil, and avoid utilities.

When street trees and open-space maintenance are the focus, evaluate all lands and trees (through a master plan design process) to review maintenance needs and get an overview of maintenance requirements. The selection of plant material is another area of potential cost savings. For example, instead of planting ordinary and inexpensive Japanese or Chinese Yews which have to be pruned 3 or 4 times a year, plant English Spreading or Greenwave Yews which maintain a height of 2 or 3 feet and need pruning once every year or two. Instead of planting Silver or Red Maple—they are rapid growers but break apart at every storm—plant 'Celebration' Maple instead. Celebration is a hybrid that combines all the positive features of both its parents and minimizes the negative features of the Red and Silver Maples.

In every new construction project, the person responsible for the landscape maintenance should make every effort to consult with the person creating the design. The plans should be checked for maintenance-saving improvements, species, or cultivars, and they must have provisions for maintenance and service equipment.

Maintenance Zones

All the workloads should be carefully planned and evaluated by the supervisor of the municipal forestry department. During this process, the workload should be divided up into maintenance zones. Assign employees to these zones so the supervisor in charge determines work assignments within the guidelines prepared by the field supervisor. This is a great morale and productivity booster. The crew knows what has to be done and when, and they have the resources to do it as efficiently as possible.

Also assign as many employees as possible to field stations in their zones where time clocks, tools, and vehicles are stored. This eliminates daily trips back and forth to the central garage and allows workers to start the day close to the job instead of waiting for a daily assignment and then driving to the site.

Tree Crews

The use of an aerial lift truck is the best way to improve tree trimming efficiency. Three or four tree climbers are needed to do what one climber and a truck can accomplish.

Some specific tips to improve productivity include the following: There should be headset communications between the person in the bucket and the person on the ground and two-way radio communication between the climber and the supervisor. Send the chipping crew out 1 hour behind the trimming crew. Collect brush in a garbage packer truck. Provide a portable toilet on the job site. A backpack blower speeds street cleanup. Have a mechanic available to keep the equipment maintained and ready to use every day. Do everything possible to keep the aerial lift working every possible moment. If there is a choice between servicing the equipment at a garage and calling a mobile repair company, select the mobile company. The job will be done faster, and the aerial lift never leaves the facility. When new equipment is chosen or modified, the field personnel should have the most say.

After the crew, the equipment is the next most important feature of a productive tree crew. Equipment should be matched to the crew to generate the most productive use of an individual's time. One crew should be available to handle demand calls for every three or four crews on scheduled pruning. Communicating with the tree crew is most important. Municipal arborists must hire the best available workers; they must talk to them and listen to them. They should inspect the workers' performance very carefully and reward the tree crew with attendance at a conference or seminar, paid days off, or a recognition luncheon. Keep the crews on the predetermined pruning schedule by providing a systematic plan with completion deadlines and budget guidelines. These set goals for the workers. Having as much mechanical equipment as possible will reduce costs and speed up the pruning process. Pole pruners and saws are more productive than chain saws, even in an aerial lift. This is due to the extended reach and fewer manuevering requirements. Prune trees when they are young and easily trimmed. A perfectly branched young tree will grow up to be a perfectly branched, low-maintenance, mature tree.

Budget Tips

1. Use the greenhouse effect, summer drought losses, or any other current event to justify more money in the planting budget.

2. Ask garden clubs and other civic groups to help contribute to a tree planting fund or to help get volunteers to plant trees. Nantucket, Massachusetts, has an organization called the Nantucket Tree Fund Committee. This organization sponsors a fashion show each year, and all the proceeds go to the tree planting fund.

3. Buy small containerized trees, and use the tree planting crew to teach volunteers from civic groups where and how to plant properly.

4. Decrease the size of trees being planted so more trees can be purchased.

5. Increase the number of bare-root trees being planted as opposed

to balled-and-burlapped trees, provided the survival rate is kept high.

6. Prune wild trees into ornamental shape.

7. Transplant small wild trees to the municipal nursery or to park sites to eliminate the purchase price.

8. Shop around before bidding to be sure there are plenty of trees in the variety and size wanted. Common varieties are less expensive than scarce varieties.

9. Plant a greater number of smaller trees in the parks and residential areas where vandalism is less likely to be a problem.

10. Will state laws allow for planting a tree on private property where the homeowner will maintain it?

11. If fees are collected from homeowners to plant trees in front of their homes, increase the fee to cover the cost of maintenance or the cost of a tree for another resident wÂho cannot afford a tree.

12. Expand the supplier market by getting prices from nurseries 1000 or more miles away. The savings could more than pay the shipping costs, provided the hardiness zone matches yours.

13. Purchase in quantity and below wholesale price.

14. Combine the bid with those from other municipalities.

15. Review bid specifications to look for cost savings.

Sources of Ideas

Get new ideas from department staff, professional organizations, seminars, the tree advisory board, and professional journals.

Integrated Pest Management

Integrated pest management (IPM) is the selection, integration, and implementation of pest control based upon predicted economic, ecological, and sociological consequences. Basically, IPM is a conservative process which reduces the need to apply pesticides. IPM is also defined as a commonsense approach to pest management. It consists of several steps:

1. Identify the plant and the pest.

2. Monitor the pest population and injury level to determine if spot treatment is sufficient or widescale treatment is necessary.

3. Determine the level of injury and decide whether the injury is acceptable, whether it is purely an aesthetic problem, and whether it is an economic problem.
4. Once it is determined that treatment is necessary, do it when the pest is in active growth, before maximum damage has occurred.
5. Consider various control methods, such as the following: Is maximum use of natural pest controls and modification techniques feasible? Will sanitation and proper arboriculture solve the problem? Other controls consist of cultural controls, such as use of mulch, water, fertilizer, and crop rotation; physical controls, such as spot treatments with insecticidal soaps, oils, low-toxicity pesticides, insect traps, or frightening devices; biological controls (see Table 5-2) consisting of such things as *Bacillus thuringiensis* (BT) and pheromones. Biological controls are preferred in order to reduce dependency on chemical pesticides, resulting in a safer environment, better worker safety, and high public health value. Plant materials bred to resist certain disease and insect problems should be used along with proper diversification.
6. Other treatments concentrate on improving plant vigor, because healthy plants discourage pest attacks and a certain low level of pest attacks is normal and should be tolerated. Planting the right tree in the right place will reduce pests that might be attracted to a poor tree or a stressful site.
7. Pesticide applications that are correct for the specific pest, only on the problem areas and only as needed, should be the treatment of last resort.
8. Once a treatment has been done, IPM requires an evaluation. Has the treatment been successful? Was the timing of the treatment correct? Was the treatment the best possible combination?
9. Records should be kept and used to compare one year to the next as well as to record the effectiveness of treatments.

Despite the efforts of the NAA, 3PF (Public Pesticide Policy Foundation), ISA, and many other organizations, environmentalists will continue their steady "pecking away" to eventually ban the use of nearly every pesticide in use today. Municipal arborists should lead the way by avoiding the use of pesticides except to protect very special trees, spraying only as needed and with the safest products available.

Plan now to avoid a problem in the future. For example, municipal forestry and park professionals should plant trees in accordance with the diversification formula. Use trees that represent the latest developments tolerating urban conditions and

Table 5-2. Biological Controls

Control	Disease
Disease-resistant cultivars and disease-free stock.	Apple scar, cedar-apple rust, powdery mildew, Dutch Elm disease, hawthorn rust, crown gall, and verticillium wilt.
Low nitrogen application.	Fire blight and powdery mildew.
Water, prune and mulch, aerify soil, avoid road salt and construction injury.	Anthracnose and decline.
Avoid injury to stems, trunks, and branches.	Anthracnose, wood decay, canker.
Well-drained planting site.	Root rot and crown rot.
Sunny site, well-spaced plantings.	Anthracnose, black spot, apple scab, powdery mildew, and various fungi.
Clean planting site and disease-free soil.	Crown gall, nematodes, root rot, verticillium, and other fungi.
Destroy diseased plants, twigs, and branches.	Dutch Elm disease, oak wilt, verticillium, anthracnose, fire blight, and cankers.
Disinfect pruning tools.	Dutch Elm disease, fire blight.

pests. Follow these guidelines, even in rural areas. By the time the trees reach maturity in 20 or 30 years, they may *be* living in an urban environment; and even if they are not, it can't hurt.

IPM works very well to reduce pesticide use, eliminate abuse, and reduce employee exposure during treatments. IPM prevents abusive chemical controls yet keeps the desirable plants alive and healthy.

Systemic Tree Injections

What Are Tree Injections?

Successful control of tree pests is dependent upon delivering the pesticide to the infested parts of the tree. One of the best ways to do this is through systemic placement of pesticides in the sapstream of the tree trunk. The chemicals are translocated throughout the tree to provide protection and control of disease and pests. Fertilizer and tree growth regulators can also be systemically applied through injections. Injections should be made only into healthy xylem. Dead or diseased xylem is not functional; therefore if this condition exists, the disease or insect has rendered the tree's system nonfunctioning and beyond the help of systemic therapy.

Systemic chemical treatments may be delivered to the tree in three well-known ways: macroinjection system, implant system, and microinjection. A *macroinjection* treatment is defined as having a wound with a diameter of $\frac{3}{8}$ inch or greater and that penetrates the xylem 1 inch to several inches. In these systems, treatment is delivered by measuring and mixing the chemicals and placing the solution into a pressurized system, which in turn delivers the chemical via a manifold series of injector tees that have been tapped into predrilled holes. The chemical being used should be labeled for systemic tree injection use. Examples of macroinjection are the systems marketed by Elm Research Institute, Harrisville, NH; the Arbotect System; the root flare or root injection systems developed by Kondo; Source Technology Biologicals' Phyton fungicide; and the Medi-ject Tree Inject Systems.

Acecap and Medicap *implants* are employed by C.S.I., Fremont, Nebraska. This method uses tiny cartridges of concentrated soluble powdered chemicals. When this system is used, the implant case is left inside the tree.

A *microinjection* treatment has a diameter of $\frac{3}{16}$ inch or smaller and penetrates the xylem $\frac{3}{4}$ inch or less. An example of a microinjection system is that developed by J. J. Mauget Co., Los Angeles, California. In this technique a feeder tube with a diameter of $\frac{11}{64}$ inch or smaller is driven into the xylem. A closed-system capsule containing the desired chemical is attached to this feeder tube, to allow the material to enter the tree. The chemicals that are available from Mauget include insecticides, fungicides, nutrients, and antibiotics.

Pros

Systemic treatments in the trunk can provide a quick therapeutic response and hold certain elements in storage for the tree's future use, and they are especially useful where conventional treatments are ineffective. Systemics are useful where environmental concerns dictate that sprays not be used. Minute quantities of chemicals are systematically delivered into the target tree without exposing the surrounding environment. The results of the injection can be seen in the tree's response in 2 to 4 weeks. There is also the advantage that systemic treatments will not harm the applicator or create pollution to the environment, wildlife, or beneficial insects. In limited applications or in treating only a few trees, it is less expensive to use systemic treatments than conventional spraying. One of the most outstanding features of systemic tree injections is the simplicity of their use by trained arborists.

Besides the avenue of injection, tree wounding is caused by pruning, mechanical damage, animals, birds, ice, insects, and human carelessness. Tree wounds for systemic treatments should be as small as possible and made in the tree's healthy tissue. Research indicates that when treatment sites have been correctly drilled and placed, most trees effectively compartmentalize the injured tissues into narrow columns of discolored wood, with little or no other permanent damage to the rest of the tree. Research has also shown no evidence of any harmful organisms entering treatment sites; and if the manufacturer's instructions are followed, the wound sites will close in the first growing season. Introduction of pesticides or fertilizer through the tree's roots generally requires incorporation of the material into the soil. Soil applications are less efficient, normally take longer, and can possibly contaminate the groundwater.

Cons

Systemic injections wound a tree. The wounds compartmentalize, and these areas of the tree cease to function. Damage from these wounds does not become visible until the tree has died and is dissected. Experiments show that abuses such as slant hole drilling, deep drilling to as much as 2.5 inches, using high-pressure pumps, and an extended period of injections can cause considerable discoloration and cell degradation. Certain injection processes that use carbon dioxide to increase pressure to force the chemicals into the tree have been known to cause considerable damage, including internal separation of growth rings and trunk splitting above and below the injection site. Each injection also creates a wound that is a potential colonization site for decay fungi. Foliar applications of materials such as pesticides, fertilizers, and fungicides avoid the need to wound trees. However, many foliar substances are slowly absorbed and poorly translocated from the leaves.

History of Tree Injections

In 1956, J. J. Mauget developed the first successful commercial injection, using a ½-inch drill and a double row of holes around a tree's trunk. In the following years, the hole size decreased dramatically, and the success of the systemic chemical treatments continued. In the early 1960s, Mauget refined the injection process, and in 1964 Shell Chemical introduced Bidrin, which Mauget put in a capsule for control of Dutch Elm disease. The capsules were pressurized 5 to 10 pounds by compression, and they were placed every 4 to 6 inches around the tree. The capsules were attached to feeder tubes which were drilled into the active xylem tissues. The systemic fluids of the tree carried and diluted the pesticide.

In 1971, Dr. Eugene Smalley, a plant pathologist, and others worked with water suspensions of benomyl fungicide. This procedure was used to combat DED and led to current low-pressure systems presently used to deliver fungicides or plant growth regulators.

It was also in 1971 that systemic implants were introduced to effectively treat iron chlorosis. Various Medicap implants became available to treat specific microelement deficiencies or to systemically fertilize trees. Recent introduction of implants containing acephate, under the trade name Acecap, allows for control of a wide range of destructive tree insects.

In 1969, Dale Dodds, a chemist-engineer, bought the Mauget Company and refined the process even more. There are many new, approved products for use by injection. For example, injections have been used successfully to treat deficiencies in iron, zinc, and manganese. Response to treatment can be evident as soon as 3 weeks, and retreatment may be required only every 3 to 5 years. Insecticide products containing Meta Systex, fertilizer offered under the name Injectamin or Stemix, and fungicide and antibiotics under the names Fungisol and Injectamycin are available from Mauget. Tree growth regulators such as Clipper were approved for limiting line trimming needs in 1982.

Field test experience in 1973 pointed to the fact that lower pressure permitted greater amounts of the fluid to enter the tree than higher pressure did.

Injection Processes

The major reason that materials can be delivered into the xylem of trees is because the pressure in the xylem, for most of the growing season, is below atmospheric pressure. Under these conditions, small amounts of chemical materials will be drawn up and into the trees due to a negative pressure gradient. If the desired site of action is the upper crown, it is best to inject during active transpiration; attempts to move materials into the roots can be accomplished best in the fall or spring. The tree soon begins to compartmentalize, however, so uptake of injected materials must occur quickly.

Current microinjection techniques require a $^{11}/_{64}$-inch-diameter hole or $^{7}/_{64}$-inch hole in certain cases, $^{3}/_{8}$ inch deep into the sapwood at or near the root flare. Root flares are areas of active growth, and correctly drilled injection holes, in these areas, usually close within one full growing season, with new tissue forming over the holes in succeeding years to restore a continuous annual ring. When correctly drilled, most trees compartmentalize the injured tissues into narrow columns of discolored wood with little or no permanent damage beyond the compartmentalized area.

Bleeder trees such as maples and birches should not be injected until the leaves are fully developed and have begun to transpire. Vessel size is one characteristic that has been related to the rate of uptake. Trees with large-diameter vessels such as oaks, elms, and ash will usually allow rapid uptake of injected materials while trees with small-diameter vessels such as maples, birches, and beeches will allow slower uptake. Additional time should be planned for treatment of those trees with small vessels.

Resin flow into injection holes of conifers may interfere with the uptake of materials. Once a systemic treatment is made, resin begins to flow into the holes as a protective response to the wounding. Resin plugging can be minimized by carefully drilling the holes, using very sharp drill bits, and inserting each feeder tube or implant within seconds after the drill wound is made. Resin plugging has not been a deterrant when the implant system is used, and the rapid uptake of materials from microinjection capsules occurs before these sites are filled with resins. Capsules left on trees for a long time, however, will fill with resin.

Thick bark can confuse the arborist, especially in species such as tulip tree, poplar, and some pines, where the inner bark is light-colored and appears to be wood. Closely examine the drill shavings for xylem wood fibers, as the drill bit is removed from the tree. Also be sure to remove all the drill shavings before inserting the feeder tube or implant capsule. It is also recommended that injections be placed in bark furrows where bark is thinnest.

Some tips to consider: Keep the holes as small and clean as possible; drill with sharp tools as low on the tree as possible; avoid vertical alignment of holes from previous treatments; remove external fixtures as soon after treatment as possible; inject only those substances that have been proved effective and noninjurious to the tree; keep the injection pressure as low as possible; and use a specialized and experienced crew. Damage to the tree will be minimized if these precautions are followed.

Descriptions of Systems

Apparatus is required for injecting systemic plant growth regulator and fungicides into the tree under high pressure. Macroinjection holes are first bored into the tree trunk to the depth of the outer layers of sapwood. Then a series of T-shaped nozzles are connected to one another with tubing and then to a container retaining the chemical solution, which must be mixed and prepared by the arborist. A high-pressure hose capable of building pressures to 400 pounds per square inch is connected to complete the system. Only experienced professional arborists should use this apparatus because tree injury is likely to occur.

The Acecap or Medicap implant technique utilizes tiny bullet-sized plastic cartridges which contain dry, water-soluble chemicals. The chemicals are absorbed into the sapstream liquid and are released, to be distributed to the tree crown. Implants are easy to use and eliminate the need to dispose of a chemical container since the implant is left inside the tree.

The Mauget microinjection system consists of a small, plastic closed capsule containing fertilizer, fungicide, insecticide, or antibiotics and a short plastic tube inserted into a predrilled hole at the base of the trunk or root flare. Installing the injector units requires some knowledge and practice. Accordingly, these are used by arborists, nursery workers, and horticulturists who have participated in a special training course.

Materials Used in Tree Injections

Microinjection capsules are used to inject liquid fertilizer directly into a tree's sapstream. This method, if employed when trees are in full leaf, bypasses the roots and begins to provide immediate help to nutritionally starved trees. This method of correcting nutritional deficiencies is particularly useful for problem trees, where successful correction cannot be produced by foliar or soil feeding. Fertilizers or agricultural minerals used by direct injection must be carefully selected for type and strength so as to be compatible with the tree. They contain specially formulated amounts of nitrogen, phosphorus, potassium, iron, zinc, copper, manganese, and essential microelements. However, the arborist must make some critical decisions regarding when the tree can be most effectively treated, which product or program should be used, and whether injection or some other treatment is required.

At effective concentrations, some fungicides promptly move into the xylem and are diluted by the fluids of the tree, to remain at an effective level while translocating throughout the trunk, branches, twigs, and leaves. If it is also phloem-mobile, the fungicide moves downward to be totally systemic within the tree's vascular system. It has been determined that during a 30-day period the concentration of fungicides in the root crown builds to and remains at a significant level. This helps explain why it has been successful against such difficult-to-control soilborne fungi as fusarium, verticillium, and others. The control of bacterial diseases such as fire blight on ornamental pear and wetwood (slime flux) on ash, elm, and oak has been well established with streptomycin injections.

The injection process is an effective means of control of insect pests that damage trees. The most widely used products are highly concentrated grades of organophosphate systemic insecticides. When injected directly into the tree's sapstream, the products move through the tree into the branches and leaves. The compound is toxic only to those insects feeding on the tree.

Guidelines

Depending on the type of tree, weather conditions, transpiration rate of the tree, soil moisture, and time of year, the uptake of chemicals may take minutes to hours. Adverse weather conditions that halt spraying can be ideal for systemic treatments. For example, in windy conditions, when spraying operations must be curtailed, fluids are lost more quickly from the leaves, internal circulation speeds up to replace the loss, and systemically applied chemicals often translocate more rapidly.

When several systemic treatment periods may be necessary, create patterns that will avoid vertical alignment of future treatment sites. Implement a tree care program that will increase the growth rate of treated trees. Proper watering, fertilizing, and pruning help keep the tree canopy demand in balance with the ability of the main stem, roots, and landform to supply. Carefully consider the wisdom of not retreating a tree if previous wounds have not closed satisfactorily after one growing season or if fluxing or cracking occurs at the treatment site. Not all trees can tolerate systemic chemicals or the physical wounding. Do not place treatment sites in the valleys between root flares where cambial growth is narrow and less conductive, and do not inject into tree roots. Follow the manufacturer's label recommendations and any supplemental guides. Correct and carefully placed treatments pay dividends in restored tree vitality. Where and when possible, monitor all treated trees and keep good records. Be sure of the source of the problem, and treat accordingly. Systemic chemical treatments are not a cure-all and require the same diagnosis and proper selection of product as when conventional spray methods are used.

Leaf Collection and Composting

Leaf Collection

Autumn leaf collection is often the job of municipal arborists, especially those employed with a Department of Public Works. Leaf collection is extremely labor-intensive and controversial in many locations because of its cost. Yard wastes consisting of leaves, animal manure, wood, and grass clippings can total 20 percent of a community's total solid waste. State and federal laws are mandating that these yard wastes be composted instead of added to the landfill or incinerated. This is resulting in a surge in composting facilities. All municipalities will soon have to have some form of composting program and operation.

There are many programs and methods of composting. For example, a 14-day compost is good for small amounts of domestic yard waste material. This is accomplished with a rotating barrel that contains fresh green grasses or leaf clippings and is rotated every 2 or 3 days. By contrast, static composting involves simply making a pile of leaves and letting them decompose without any management. This process requires 2 to 3 years and involves anaerobic decomposition, which creates odor problems.

There are many alternative programs between these two extremes. Many communities actively encourage residents to develop backyard composting areas to keep leaves and grass from ever getting into the wastestream. Many other communities pick up leaves and grass in special bags or on special trucks run on the same day as other curbside collection. This solid waste is then processed at a municipal compost operation center.

Leaf loader. (*Courtesy Ford New Holland, Inc.*)

The major factor to reduce the municipal cost of picking up yard wastes is to increase mechanization and to decrease labor. The leaf collection process can be the biggest and most costly municipal operation during each October and November. The process consists of raking leaves into windrows or piles along the street where they can be loaded for removal. The rows are generally made by residents and modified by laborers working with rakes. The rows can also be made with blowers. Rakers are the limiting factor in the speed of leaf removal operations. Two rakers can usually cover 4 to 6 curb-miles per day.

The type of row or pile depends upon the type of machine available for picking up the leaves. For example, vacuum machines—self-contained, tow-behind, or attached to a truck—all work best for picking up windrows or piles. Vacuums also reduce the leaf volume by 5 times, but they do not work as well when the leaves are wet. There are new machines that bale the leaves like hay, baler-like machines that pick up the leaves and blow them into trucks, and auger machines that work like snow blowers. All these machines also work best by picking leaves up from windrows. *The Claw* is an attachment to a loader that works by squeezing a pile between two "arms" prior to lifting it into the truck. Some cities use a trash packer in combination with The Claw to accept the leaves and haul them to the compost pile. The packer also compresses leaves to approximately half the volume of the pile in the street. Front-end loaders and street sweepers are slow but work well if the leaf piles are wet or frozen. Street sweepers are also an asset for the cleanup of loose leaves and dirt on the street following any type of street leaf cleanup.

There are many modifications to these ideas that make leaf collection a very local and individualized program. One very successful program sells permits to commercial landscape maintenance companies. The landscapers are then allowed to bring leaves to a special dump site in unlimited trips. The permit fees are placed in a special account and are spent on piling the leaves into windrows for composting. The fee also covers the total, one-year cost of managing the composting operations and the final screening of the finished leaf mold.

Other modifications include having residents collect the leaves and deliver them to compost areas or satellite areas where the municipality operates a transfer or compost operation. This eliminates costs to the municipality for pickup of the leaves. The use of biodegradable plastic or paper bags is questionable. Communities have found that bags do not decompose as readily as the leaves, which increases the composting time and decreases the quality of the finished leaf mold. If twigs, bags, or wood chips are added to the composting operation, the composting time is extended by as much as an additional 6 to 12 months.

Composting

The making of composted leaf mold is actually a simple process, but a thorough knowledge of the process is required to ensure success. The choice of composting site is often a political decision and one that is often met with neighborhood opposition. This opposition comes from a lack of understanding about how the composting process works. One often used argument deals with leachate. However, leaves, grass clippings, and wood chips or wood debris do not create leachate problems. Animal manure wastes, while providing nutrients to the compost, could cause leachate problems. Another complaint deals with odor. However, a properly managed leaf composting operation does not generate any offensive odor or rodent problems, so there is no reason for complaint. The composting site can be a former landfill, unused park, or vacant land. The site must have a total acreage that will equal approximately 1 acre of compost site per square mile of municipality or 1 acre per 30 miles of streets, whichever is less. It is more efficient to operate the entire operation at one site, but in the larger cities this is not always feasible. If residents are expected to deliver leaves to the site themselves, the site needs to be accessible to most everyone in the municipality. If the municipality operates a citywide cleanup, then access is less important.

The site should be gently sloping, well-drained, and hard. Surface drainage should not go directly into brooks or catch basins but into a retention basin or should percolate into the ground first. The site should be on a constant slope and open, so there is room to maneuver equipment and store the leaves. The leaves should be piled in windrows that are as long or as wide as the available site and as high as the municipal equipment (loaders) can reach while maintaining the piles. The pile should be as wide as it is high. The piles should go up and down the slope so rainwater is not trapped by the pile. The windrows are designed to let air and moisture enter the pile. One tip many communities take advantage of is to build twin windrows when the leaves are being delivered to the site; then at the first turning of the piles, they are combined into one. Since the most rapid leaf size reduction occurs in the first month, the twin piles can easily be managed as one large pile after that first month. As a general rule of thumb, 1000 cubic yards of leaves on the street will eventually become about 200 yards of composted leaf mold.

Size reduction can also be accomplished by mechanically shredding the leaves prior to composting. Shredding will reduce the time to complete the composting process by almost 50 percent. Shredded leaves can also be used as a mulch without composting. Unfortunately, the leaves have to be replaced annually, and the decomposition process has been known to rob the soil and plants of nutrients. Large pieces of shredded leaves can also be blown away if the landscaped area is windy.

Ingredients and Procedures

The following are all the necessary steps to ensure successful composting.

1. *Air.* Ideally, perforated pipes should be run through the compost pile. A more practical solution is to loosely stack the leaves in long, narrow rows, using a front-end loader. Oxygen is essential to preventing anaerobic decomposition and promoting aerobic composting.

2. *Turning.* Turning the pile mixes the materials, reaerates the compost, and provides a check on the progress of composting. Frequent turning speeds composting. The minimum interval is 4 days; the more practical is 1 month.

3. *Nutrients.* It is very important to feed nitrogen to the composting bacteria. The best means is to add manure to the compost during the turning procedure. If manure is unavailable or not allowed, the next best sources of nitrogen are weeds, grass clippings, aquatic weeds, and commercial nitrogen fertilizer. All but the fertilizer also supply the heat required for composting (see step 5).

4. *Bacteria.* Commercial bacterial compost starters are available; however, the occasional mixing of compost with previously composted garden soil should provide sufficient quantities of bacteria seed. If the same site is used year after year, the bacteria can be obtained by scrapping up the top inch or two of soil when the pile is turned over the first and second times. After the composting action has begun, additional bacteria do not need to be added.

5. *Heat.* The optimum temperature is 140°F (60°C). This is no problem in summer, but composting over winter requires special insulation with hay or uncomposted leaves, which will also protect the pile from winter rains. When the temperature has cooled to 100°F, the compost action is finished. Weeds, green vegetation, and manure speed up the heating and composting action. The top 3 feet of surface area are unlikely to decompose as readily as the interior of the pile. Therefore, when the pile is turned, exteriors should be moved to the center of the new pile and the centers moved out to cure at the edge.

6. *Moisture.* Rainfall is generally sufficient, but a sprinkler may be necessary to supplement natural rainfall and to ensure a wet but not dripping condition.

Turning the pile on a rainy day allows moisture to be mixed throughout the entire pile. It also provides an opportunity to utilize equipment that would normally be used on other outdoor projects. If the piles are close to residential neighbors, rainy-day turning takes advantage of the fact that neighbors' windows are likely to be closed because of the rain and the chance for odor release will not cause any complaints. This makes for good neighbors, which also keeps political leaders happy.

As the composting action proceeds, the pH value fluctuates from acidic in the beginning to neutral at completion. When the compost cycle is completed, the windrow can be screened and piled to cure. Curing allows the compost to stabilize so nutrients are released when the compost is added to the garden instead of consumed by bacteria and depleted by continued decomposition.

The uses of composted leaf mold are many. It can be mixed with one-third compost, one-third sand, and one-third soil to create topsoil. It can be substituted for peat, any time peat is required in construction, or for greenhouse potting soil. It makes an excellent top dressing for turf areas and mulch in a garden. It is an excellent cover for construction restoration. Many communities with successful composting operations no longer purchase topsoil. Other communities sell the material to topsoil companies, greenhouses, nurseries, garden shops, and residents or use the material as incentives for sales of other surplus products, such as wood chips and lumber from forestry operations. Some communities have a Give-Away Day to get rid of their surplus leaf mold. Others sell it for $10 per yard, screened and delivered.

A successful leaf composting operation requires careful attention to and planning of the site selection, the collection system, management of materials, utilization of the product, and community involvement and support.

Disposal of Wood and Chips

Disposal of tree trimmings and wood debris is a major problem for municipalities and their forestry departments. Most trimming material is generally reduced to wood chips by chippers that are towed behind the aerial lifts or chip trucks. There are several creative ways to dispose of the chips as well as wood and stumps that are too large for the chipper.

Wood chips are most easily utilized by municipal park and landscape departments for mulch. Chips may also be made available to residents, golf courses, and botanical gardens. Chips can be made smaller and then added to the compost pile. Chips

Top: Leaf composting in windrow. *Bottom:* Wood chip compost, shredded.

coming from brush are generally too poor in quality for anything but composting. Sometimes the chips can be sold as fuel or as a bulking agent for a sewage treatment plant's aerobic composting operations. Agricultural communities can use wood chips as bedding for animals and poultry. Some chips can be used for making particle board and paper products. Some communities have programs where residents can have a load of chips delivered to the driveway. The residents are encouraged to use the chips to spread around the base of their trees. This mulch protects the tree trunks from mower damage while also conserving moisture, insulating the soil from temperature extremes, and keeping weeds from competing for nutrients with the tree.

The disposal of wood logs entails different problems. Most small logs, 3 to 8 inches in diameter, can be used as firewood. Some residents may take larger pieces and split them up if the wood is desirable firewood and is cut into 2-foot lengths. Wood larger than 8 inches, however, is generally not usable. Especially, since most street trees are not removed until absolutely necessary, there is often a lot of rot in the trunk. Sometimes the rot has been replaced with concrete or brick. Even logs without rot might contain nails that were left in the tree many years ago. All this makes the wood useless for saw logs and undesirable for firewood. However, this wood can be chipped, provided a machine is available in the municipality that can handle larger wood. In any event, the cost to dispose of the logs is high.

With the use of coal, fuel oil, and natural gas predominating for heating purposes, it may be useful to compare a fuel to wood. A cord of dry hardwood of mixed species weighs 2 tons and is equivalent to a ton of coal or 160 to 170 gallons of fuel oil.

Disposal of stumps is best done by grinding the stump where it sits in the ground. Stumping machines are available at reasonable cost and can dispose of 90 percent of the stumps in a municipal forestry operation. The stumps that are dug must be buried in a landfill or stump dump, if permits can be obtained. The only other viable solution is to use a whole-tree chipper to reduce the stump to chips. These high-priced machines are available for purchase or rental. The disposal of vines and brush is often difficult with chippers. Disposal of this debris is better done with a tub grinder. Unfortunately, most tub grinders cannot handle large wood, logs, or stumps as well as a whole-tree chipper does.

Occasionally trees of value are removed. The municipal arborist should salvage cedar or hickory wood chips and clear logs if they become available. Toledo, Ohio, for example, sells hickory wood

Comparison of Coal in Tons to a Cord of Dry Wood

Chipping branches. (*Courtesy Donald G. Yates.*)

Wood and brush
harvesting. *Top:*
Loading. *Middle:*
Compressing. *Bottom:*
Chipping.

Comparison of Coal in Tons to a Cord of Dry Wood

1 cord of	Equals
Shagbark Hickory	1.36 ton(s) of coal
White Oak	1.26
Beech	1.20
Yellow Birch	1.18
Sugar Maple	1.18
Red Oak	1.18
White Ash	1.10
Red Maple	1.02
American Elm	0.93
Aspen	0.69
White Pine	0.67

chips to residents who add them to their barbecue fires. Toledo has a small sawmill which cuts large logs into boards, and the lumber is sold on demand. Oak and walnut boards are the most popular woods. Toledo also sells firewood with the price depending upon whether it is split or not split. Certain woods such as cottonwood, boxelder, and willow are free for the taking. Photos of the Toledo operation are on the next page.

The basic way of disposing of all wood products is to be creative and find a way that works best for you and your community.

Sources

ACRT: *Vancouver Street Tree Plan*, Kent, OH, 1990.

American National Standards Institute: *Pruning, Trimming, etc. Safety Requirements*, ANSI Z133.1-1988.

"Arbor Day/Earth Day 1990," *City Trees*, March/April 1990, p. 12.

"Arbor Day Programs, 1990," *City Trees*, May/June 1990, p. 5.

Bieller, John A.: "Injection Site Wounding When Using Plant Growth Regulators," *Journal of Arboriculture*, 17(3): 78–79, March 1991.

Boerner, Deborah A.: "Nurturing New Trees," *Urban Forests*, June/July 1990, p. 9.

Boers, Richard W.: "Toledo, Ohio, City of the Month," *City Trees*, September/October 1990, pp. 6–7.

Bridgemen, P. H.: *Tree Surgery, A Complete Guide*, David and Charles, Inc., North Pomfret, Vermont, 1977.

Wood utilization. *Top:* Special hickory wood chips. *Middle:* Sawmill operation. *Bottom:* Splitting firewood.

Bulpitt, Stan: *Municipal Leaf Composting: A Solid Waste Recycling Program*, Royer Foundry, Kingston, PA, 1973.

Cornell University, Ithaca, NY, *Conservation Circular*, 6(1), January 1968.

Costonis, Arthur C.: "Tree Injection, Perspective Macro-Injection/Micro-Injection," *Journal of Arboriculture*, 7(10): 275–277, October 1981.

Davey Resource Group: *Community Forest Management in Longview, OR*. Irvine, CA, 1991.

diSalvo, Carol: "Practical I.P.M. Programs," *City Trees*, January/February 1990, p. 19.

Dodds, Dale I.: "Tree Care: Helping Nature with Science," *Weeds, Trees and Turf*, January 1974, p. 14.

Dykema, Paul: *City of Lansing Forestry Section Master Plan*, City of Lansing, MI, 1991.

Hartman, John: "Controlling Diseases in Landscape Plants," *Landscape Management*, May 1991, p. 38.

"Innovations in Park Management and Municipal Arboriculture," *City Trees*, January/February 1991, p. 8.

Kielbaso, J. James, Davidson, Harold, Hart, John, Jones, Alan, and Kennedy, M. Keith: *Symposium on Systemic Chemical Treatments in Tree Culture*, Michigan State University, East Lansing, 1978.

Krause, David: "Root Barriers and Tree Growth Regulators," *City Trees*, March/April 1991, p. 14.

Mah-Kooyman, Shirley: "Volunteers," *City Trees*, January/February 1991, p. 18.

Massachusetts, Commonwealth of: *Municipal Leaf Composting*, Boston, 1987.

J. J. Mauget Company: *Scientific and Effective Tree Care*, Los Angeles, n.d.

Miller, Dr. Robert W.: *Urban Forestry, Planning and Managing Urban Greenspaces*, Prentice-Hall, Englewood Cliffs, NJ, 1988.

National Arborist Association: *Pruning Standards for Shade Trees*, Amherst, NH 1988.

Neely, Dan: "Implants Correct Iron Deficiency," *Journal of Forestry*, June 1973, p. 6.

Neely, Dan: "Tree Wound Closure," *Journal of Arboriculture*, 14(6), June 1988, pp. 148–152.

Nowak, David J.: "Street Tree Pruning and Removal Needs," *Journal of Arboriculture*, 16(12): 309–315, December 1990.

Phillips, Leonard E., Jr.: "Budget Time," *City Trees*, January/February 1991, p. 6.

Phillips, Leonard E., Jr.: "Solution to the Greenhouse Effect," *City Trees*, January/February 1989, p. 4.

Phillips, Leonard E., Jr.: "Design for Maintenance," *City Trees*, April 1986, p. 13.

Phillips, Leonard E., Jr.: "It's the Little Things that Count," *City Trees*, October 1985, p. 11.

Phillips, Leonard E., Jr.: "Leaf Composting Procedures," Wellesley Department of Public Works, Wellesley, MA, July 1979.

Pirone, P. P., Hartman, J. R., Sall, M. A., and Pirone, T. P.: *Tree Maintenance*, 6th ed., Oxford University Press, New York, 1988.

Plowman, Vic: "Tree Injections—Products, Safety and

Feasibility," *City Trees*, March 1991, p. 4.

"Results of the Readers' Survey about Innovative Ideas," *City Trees*, May/June 1988, p. 10.

Schroeder, Jennifer: "Sidewalks and Tree Roots," *City Trees*, March/April 1991, p. 13.

Shigo, Alex L.: *A New Tree Biology*, Shigo and Trees, Durham, NH, 1989.

Shigo, Alex L.: *Injections and Injury*, Northeastern Forest Experiment Station, Durham, NH, n.d.

Smith, Deborah, and Starton Gill: "Anatomy of an IPM Program," *Landscape Management*, August 1987, p. 46.

Tatter, Terry A.: "Minimizing Uptake Problems during Micro-Injection," *Scientific Tree Care with Micro-Injection Technology*, Farm and Forest Research Co., Ltd., Oakville, Ontario, n.d.

Watson, Dr. Gary: "Disorders Caused by Root Related Stresses," *City Trees*, September/October 1990, p. 15.

Webb, R. E., Reardon, R. C., Wieber, A. M., Boyd, V. K., Larew, H. G., and Argauer, R. J.: "Suppression of Gypsy Moth Populations on Oak Using Implants or Injections, etc.," *Journal of Economic Entomology*, 81(2), April 1988, pp. 573–577.

Endnote

Special thanks for technical assistance to Nathan Dodds (J. J. Mauget), Arnold Ferran (consulting arborist), and Warren Wolfe (Creative Sales, Inc.).

6
Administration

Municipal Forestry Departments

The municipal arborist is responsible for the management of the urban forest in his or her community. To accomplish this task, the arborist needs trained and qualified help to manage the trees, operate the equipment, and perform a multitude of other tasks "as required." All the employees are hired under the direction of the arborist or an administrator, and the entire department is organized according to the local policies, budget, size of the department, and size of the municipality.

Department Organization

The smallest cities might have a forester who writes tree maintenance contracts or a forestry division consisting of two or three workers plus a truck who report to a city leader or department head. Moderate-size communities and departments might have two crews consisting of two climbers, two truck drivers, and a foreman who might serve as the supervisor.

As the size of the city and the number of urban trees increase, so do the size and the complexity of the urban forestry department. The organizational charts of three cities are illustrated on pages 121 and 122. The largest cities have several trimming crews, each working in a certain zone or section of the city. They might also have a trouble truck used to trim limbs that are blocking signs or hazardous limbs that hang over walks and streets. Sometimes this crew is called a *request trimming crew*. This crew takes care of trees needing attention according to phone calls from residents and political leaders. Other crews can be assigned to tree planting during spring and fall planting seasons and to tree removal at other times of the year. Other crews may be assigned to pest control and to implement IPM and other insect and disease control programs. The tree watering personnel, who usually follow the planting crew, are also essential to protecting the community's investment in its trees.

All the crews should have leaders who stay with the workers to supervise the work and answer questions from the public and field supervisors who go from crew to crew and report directly to the arborist or department head. All the daily assignments are also flexible and will vary in size and need, depending upon the season, weather, and job assignment.

In larger cities, usually one to several urban foresters are in charge of the field supervisors, who direct the foremen, who in turn direct the workers. This is called the *chain of command.* Every smooth operation has a clear line of communication that flows up and down the chain. Chains that operate properly prevent mistakes and misunderstandings both up and down the chain. A good organization also effectively utilizes the department's resources and controls employee assignments. A good organizational chart describes the functions of the personnel, duties, and lines of communication. The organization should be loose enough that employees can be moved to best match their personalities and skills with the assignments.

Also in larger cities the Forestry Department is usually a division or bureau within another department such as the Parks, Public Works, or Street Department. There are as many different department organizations as there are departments across the United States and Canada. Most forestry departments have an advisory board which sets policy and regulations that the department must follow. The advisory board is usually composed of volunteers who are interested in promoting urban forestry. They are often invaluable in supporting the forestry budget, attending Arbor Day functions, and helping to plant trees.

Department Standards

The Forestry Department Accreditation program by the Society of Municipal Arborists sets a series of standards that a department must meet to be accredited. These standards help to define the "ideal" professional forestry department. Some of these standards include the following: There should be a maximum of 10,000 street trees per tree climber employed by the forestry department. All trees should be pruned within a maximum 10-year cycle. Each climber should receive a minimum of 20 hours of forestry and pesticide training per year, including training in aerial rescue plus cardiopulmonary resuscitation (CPR) and first-responder training.

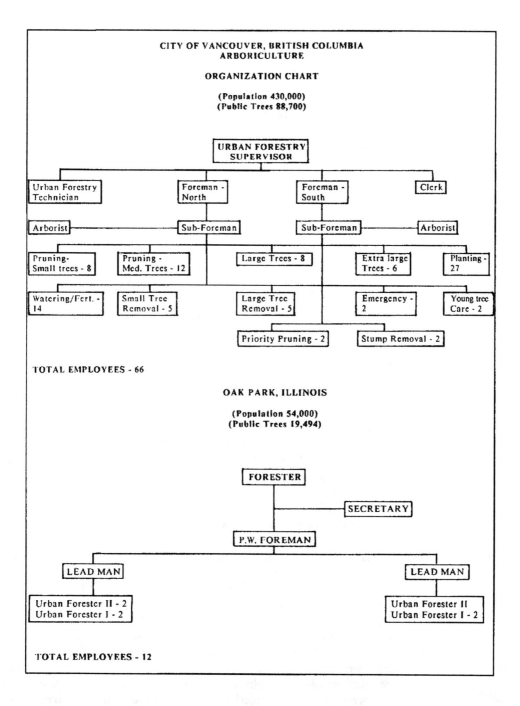

CITY OF VANCOUVER, BRITISH COLUMBIA
ARBORICULTURE

ORGANIZATION CHART

(Population 430,000)
(Public Trees 88,700)

URBAN FORESTRY SUPERVISOR

Urban Forestry Technician | Foreman - North | Foreman - South | Clerk

Arborist — Sub-Foreman | Sub-Foreman — Arborist

Pruning- Small trees - 8 | Pruning - Med. Trees - 12 | Large Trees - 8 | Extra large Trees - 6 | Planting - 27

Watering/Fert. - 14 | Small Tree Removal - 5 | Large Tree Removal - 5 | Emergency - 2 | Young tree Care - 2

Priority Pruning - 2 | Stump Removal - 2

TOTAL EMPLOYEES - 66

OAK PARK, ILLINOIS

(Population 54,000)
(Public Trees 19,494)

FORESTER

SECRETARY

P.W. FOREMAN

LEAD MAN | LEAD MAN

Urban Forester II - 2
Urban Forester I - 2 | Urban Forester II
Urban Forester I - 2

TOTAL EMPLOYEES - 12

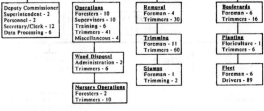

CITY OF CHICAGO, ILLINOIS
BUREAU OF FORESTRY

ORGANIZATION CHART

(Population 2,783,726)
(Public Trees 440,943)

TOTAL EMPLOYEES - 371

At least one employee in ten should have a pesticide license if one is available from the state.

Some other accreditation standards apply to the budget. For example, less than 30 percent of the budget should be spent for tree removals and for administration, while a minimum of 30 percent is required for trimming and 5 percent for planting. At least $2.00 per capita is required to have a total budget that is adequate to support proper tree maintenance. Within the total budget, an amount of $0.01 per capita should be set aside for tree research. Time allocation or labor distribution requires that a minimum of 50 percent of the total labor hours be spent on pruning, but there is a maximum of 25 percent labor on emergency work and 30 percent on demand pruning.

The accreditation standards go on to qualify the municipal arborist. The arborist should be a full-time employee having a college degree in forestry or a related field. She or he should be a member of and attend at least one meeting per year of an arboricultural organization. The arborist also should have at least 5 hours of training per year and should become certified by the ISA.

Training programs, mentioned above, can vary widely for forestry employees. The simplest consists of slide and cassette shows held at the field office on rainy days. These programs are available from the National Arborists Association as well as other commercial training companies, and they provide information on tree care, pesticide application, safety, etc. Other training consists of sending employees to local universities or trade associations where they can attend everything from lectures and seminars to courses on all subjects related to the field. On-the-job training and visitation to other municipal departments provide training in a practical sense.

Inviting lecturers to visit with films and talks also provide good training. Employees should be encouraged to attend trade shows and to belong to professional organizations. Employees should also have subscriptions to trade journals and access to various books that will keep them up to date. Where pesticide licenses are required, employees usually take several refresher courses. Every forestry employee should participate in some of these training programs wherever they are available.

Employee Assistance Programs

Managing employees can be difficult at times. The consequences of alcoholism and drug abuse in the workplace are seen in lowered productivity, increased absenteeism, inefficiency, increased turnover, increased injury rates, and incidents arising from behavioral problems. Employees with these problems can be disruptive and demoralizing to others, and this leads to excessive turnover.

Many municipalities believe that employees with alcohol or drug problems require professional assistance. Early recognition of these conditions by the employer is key to an effective program of evaluation, treatment, and rehabilitation. Concern with alcoholism and drug abuse is a basic management responsibility. Supervisors are expected to be familiar with employees' appearance, behavior, and work patterns and to be alert to any changes. These could result from causes other than drug abuse such as illness, properly prescribed drugs, and fatigue. Supervisors are not expected to make a diagnosis; that is the responsibility of medical professionals. They are expected to point out where the troubled employee could turn.

Studies indicate that, at any one time, 10 to 20 percent of the population is taking prescription medications. Add to this the number of people using drugs illegally, and it becomes obvious that a substantial portion of the population is exposed to the effects of drugs. No matter how often you speak about the hazardous effects of alcohol, the person who enjoys drinking will continue to do so.

Identifying employees with drug and alcohol problems is much easier if the municipality takes a positive approach. Since drug and alcohol dependencies cause marked changes in work behavior, personal relations, and emotional moods, supervisors should seek the assistance of the personnel department or a community agency that deals with the treatment of drug or alcohol dependency. A municipality must also establish a written policy that conforms to the law when planning countermeasures to drug or alcohol abuse. This policy must be carefully prepared and made known to all employees in the same manner as a safety policy.

Employee assistance programs are being implemented by enlightened management to help employees with alcohol and other behavioral problems that interfere with job performance. Programs of this type enable an agency to retain valued employees.

Labor Unions

Another factor that management has to take into consideration is a labor union. Municipal arborists in management should carefully consider the value of a union and how they can manipulate negotiations to their advantage. Managers should negotiate for contracts that give freedom to manage in exchange for employee raises and benefits, for example, replacing the concept of "seniority" with "most qualified" in exchange for 5 percent raises or 3-year contracts; or earning a personal day off in exchange for no sick days taken during a quarter; or installing flexible time in exchange for hikes in the longevity bonus.

Understand exactly what can and cannot be done according to the contracts. Stretch the *can's* creatively by gradually establishing a past practice or by exercising management rights that are implied but not clearly stated. Don't be afraid of a grievance if a point will be made or management will gain substantially regardless of who wins the specific issue.

Also be sure there is flexibility in all actions. For example, during disciplinary actions, make the first suspension for 2 days so if there is a need to compromise, management can drop back to 1 day and the point will still have been made. During disciplinary actions use a progressive policy (first abuse, 2 days; second abuse, 1 week; third abuse, 1 month, and fourth abuse, termination) and document everything!

Equipment for Professional Tree Care

Proper equipment can be vital to the success of a tree care operation. Equipment can be grouped into categories such as pruning tools, safety equipment, transportation, and cleanup equipment. All tools must be kept clean and in proper working order at all times. The equipment must also conform to the safety regulations of the American National Standards Institute (ANSI). The descriptions and illustrations below provide information about only the basic equipment.

Pruning Tools

Pruning shears

Lopping shears

Pruning saw

Pole pruning saw

Axe

Pruners are used for cutting branches of up to 1-inch diameter. The anvil style has a special steel blade that cuts against a brass anvil. The hook-and-blade style is more common and has a curved anvil. Pruner carrying cases are available that can be attached to the worker's belt.

Loppers have long handles and can prune branches up to 3 inches in diameter. These special steel blades are mounted with handles of hickory, ash, or spring steel. Some loppers have gear drive to increase the cutting power.

Saws in this category are generally 20 to 26 inches long with a curved steel blade. These saws are designed to cut limbs 1 to 20 inches in diameter on the draw stroke. Pruning saws designed for larger limbs have gullets cut into the blade to carry away the dust. New high-technology cutting teeth are the best available. These super-sharp blades are dangerous and should be kept sheathed until in use. All pruning saws should be kept in a rubber, plastic, or leather scabbard. The scabbard protects the saw as well as the tree climber's legs and clothes.

The same blade on a pruning saw can be attached to a 6- or 8-foot pole and used in combination with a pruning head similar to a lopping shear. The pruning head is operated by pulley and a rope pulled at the ground level. The pole can be round, square, or octagonal with up to 3- to 6-foot extension sections. The poles can be made of wood, fiberglass, or aluminum.

The double- and single-bit axe, brush hooks, peavey, and other logging tools are seldom (if ever) used in urban forestry operations.

The chain saw is the arborist's major pruning tool. It is usually overused because of its convenience, and it affords climbers the opportunity to remove branches that are too big and to cut more than is necessary for proper tree care. Professional-grade chain saws for urban forestry use come as small as 10 pounds with 11-inch bars and go up to 20 pounds and a 42-inch bar. The saws all have safety features, easy maintenance, and long life. Some of the best common brands used in urban forestry include Jonsered, McCulloch, Homelite, Husqvarna, Poulan, and Stihl.

Chain saw

Safety Equipment

Rope used in tree care operations ranges from ½- to 1-inch diameter and is made from different types and combinations of synthetic fibers. Nylon rope has excessive stretch but is used by some for pull or lowering lines and short safety lines. Climbing ropes must have a

Rope

Lanyards

Goggles

Hard hat

Ear protection

Safety chaps

core of high tenacity such as nylon with an outer sheath of dacron, polyester, and/or polyester-coated polypropylene, and are usually ½ to ¾ inch in diameter. Combo or composite rope is inexpensive and ⅝ to 1 inch in diameter and is good for pull or lowering lines only. The rope should be long-wearing and easy to handle. Climbing rope supports the climber and must be the strongest rope available that is easy to handle. Some are waxed to prevent knot fusing.

One type of lanyard is attached to the saddle and holds the climber around the tree or as a safety device on aerial personnel lifts. These safety straps are made of nylon or rope. Other lanyards are attached between the climber and the chain saw. This lanyard is long enough to drop the saw below the climber's feet to prevent injury, if dropped.

Goggles should be worn at all times when one is working around trees. The face shield on a hard hat can be a substitute for goggles. Goggles come with stainless-steel-mesh screens or polycarbonate clear lenses. They should have an adjustable elastic headband and ventilation.

The hard hat should be made of polyethylene and meet all federal safety standards for impact and electrical hazard. It must also have an adjustable headband that keeps the top of the hat suspended at least one inch above the head. Helmets also have accessories. The hat can come with a screen visor, a face shield, and ear protectors, all built in for added safety. Winter liners keep the head warm in cold weather.

Ear protection comes in four basic types. One is foam plugs which expand to fit the ear. They cost about $0.20 each and are disposable. Plastic-coated plugs contain fibers wrapped in plastic that "breathes." They allow the wearer to hear voices, but high frequencies are filtered out. This type is also disposable and costs about $0.15 each. Insert pads have soft, cushiony pads on a thermoplastic band that goes under the chin or behind the neck. This is easy to clean and costs about $6. Muff-type hearing protectors go over the ear and are designed to filter out high-frequency sounds. The strap between the earmuffs can go over the head, behind the neck, or under the chin. The muffs can also be attached to the hard hat. Their price ranges from $8 to $22 depending on the style, features, design, and noise reduction rating.

Chaps are made to go over the trousers of the chain saw operator to protect the legs from the saw. Most chaps are made with five or six layers of nylon including three or four layers of cut-resistant Kevlar, designed to clog and stall the chain saw on impact, thus preventing the body from being cut or injured.

The saddle provides the seat for the climber and a belt where

Climbing saddle

Body/boom belts
and lanyard

Climbing spurs

Safety cones, flags,
and signs

ropes and tools can be attached. The saddle is generally made of leather and nylon. When used in combination with rope, it provides the climber with the lifeline to safety. The saddle has D rings to which the climbing rope is attached. Other tools and lanyards are also attached to the saddle.

The body belt is attached to a tree climber in a bucket truck. A lanyard connects the body belt with the upper boom. This safety device prevents the bucket operator who is thrown or knocked out of the bucket from being seriously injured.

Climbing spurs should be used seldom and then only if the tree is dead or is to be removed. Climbing spurs are leg irons with steel gaffs that penetrate the tree bark, enabling the tree climber to ascend the tree. Since each gaff mark wounds the tree, the spurs should not be used on live trees. On dead trees, the climber can be injured if the bark peels off the tree under the climber's weight. Spurs can also be cumbersome to the climber who is working in the tree. The spurs have ankle and calf straps plus a climbing pad around the calf.

This miscellaneous safety equipment is used for the protection of ground personnel and vehicular equipment. Ground personnel should also be equipped with a fluorescent safety vest for use when working in roadways.

Transportation Equipment

Aerial lift

There is a wide range of sizes and types of aerial lift. They save a great deal of time in tree trimming. Models desired for work near power lines are heavily insulated in the upper boom, lower boom, and basket liner. The lifts are articulating to provide as much as 280 degrees of operation, which gives the operator the flexibility needed to go over, under, or around wires and large limbs while pruning the trees. The lifts also come in heights from 40 to 60 feet for work in trees, although some utility lifts can work up to 130 feet tall. The most popular lifts available for urban forestry functions include Altec, Aerial Lift, Hi-Ranger, and Versalift.

The truck chassis is usually a common truck such as Ford, International, Mack, GMC, etc. It should have at least a 28,000-pound capacity with several other specifications matched to the aerial lift requirements. The truck body usually contains a chip box, tool box, and a towing package to pull a chipper. The body design, however, depends upon the local requirements and budget.

Truck

Since the personnel basket is equipped with hydraulics, the climber should have access to hydraulic saws and pruners as well as a separate chain saw. Hydraulic tools come with circular or chain saw heads and 2-inch lopper heads. The choice between these

Bucket saws

depends on the preference and skill of the operator. All the heads are hand-held or mounted on poles to increase operator productivity, and they are insulated to protect the operator from electrical accidents. Chain saw use requires more manipulation to get closer to the work site than hydraulic saws do, so chain saws are less productive. The hydraulic equipment is also much quieter and more lightweight than the chain saw.

Clean-up Equipment

Chipper

Today, there are two basic types of chippers. The drum chipper has a rotor-drum cutter head that will process large volumes of brush and branches up to 6 inches in diameter. The disk chipper will cut branches and logs up to 12 inches in diameter. The disk is generally a 40-inch flywheel with knives and a feed system to control the flow of wood entering the cutter knives. Both chipper types are generally powered with heavy-duty engines attached to the chipper trailer. They also have fans to blow the chips into the discharge chute.

Aerial lift and chip truck at work. (*Courtesy Dave Shaw.*)

Safety precautions are built into both styles of chippers, but there is no substitute for common sense and being careful around these potentially deadly tools.

Stump grinders were originally for homeowner use and were later enlarged and improved for commercial and municipal operations. The stump grinder consists of a wheel covered with carbide-tipped cutting teeth. The spinning wheel cuts the stump into wood chips. Stump grinders can be small with a 16-horsepower engine, a 14-inch wheel, and 12 teeth up to a 65+-horsepower engine, a 36-inch wheel, and 56+ teeth. The larger machine can cut up to 2 feet below the ground and a 72-inch stump. All stump grinders are designed for operator safety. Care should be taken to prevent personal injury or property damage. They will reduce a stump from 12 inches above the ground to 12 inches below the ground within a few minutes. All that is left is a pile of chips and dirt.

Lawn rakes are especially good for cleaning up wood chips, sawdust, and leaves after pruning, tree removal, or other tree work. The best lawn rakes have reinforced springs which place tension on the tines, are 24 inches wide, and have a handle at least 54 inches long.

Street brooms with long, brown plastic bristles last the longest. A 60-inch handle makes the broom more comfortable. The broom is used for the final cleanup of the piles of leaves, chips, etc. Sweeping the debris into a square, flat shovel can eliminate all the debris following a major work effort.

There are many specialty tools for guying/cabling, tree surveys, planting tools, etc. that are far too numerous to mention. The municipal arborist will know which tools are needed and must be purchased based upon his or her experience, training, and education. Many tools also have regional traditions, styles, or preferences that are also too numerous to mention.

Stumper

Rakes

Broom

Contracting versus In-House Forestry Staff

Is it less expensive to use a contractor, paid by the job, plus profit, or have in-house forestry staff, paid year-round, plus benefits? This question is often asked by most city managers as they search for ways to provide required municipal services for the lowest cost. Forestry services can be accomplished by using contractors, in-house staff, or combinations of both.

Typical contracted services include tree planting; tree growing; tree pruning; tree removals; stump grinding; wood disposal; electric line trimming; and management consultants who can do inventories, create master plans, write and oversee contracts, and prepare all types of documents and regulations.

The advantages of in-house crews include having people available to do anything and everything that needs to be done. The community also has an identity or personality that is reflected in the maintenance of its street trees. Quality control is better with in-house crews who have to live with their mistakes and be proud of their accomplishments. In-house crews can be kept busy with all phases of municipal forestry, which introduces some variety to the daily routine. In-house crews can also become specialized and just as productive as contracted labor.

In most situations, the decision to use contractors versus in-house staff versus a combination of both is usually made on the basis of cost, quality of service desired, and past practice. For example, Milwaukee has 325,000 street trees, a $4,850,000 budget, and 110 workers while Chicago has 440,943 street trees, a 1990 budget of $12,779,690, and 135 workers. Both cities do all operations with in-house crews. Cincinnati, Ohio, and Longmeadow, Massachusetts, are two examples where everything but administration is done by contract. Most cities, however, have combinations of both.

In Wellesley, Massachusetts, a recent study was prepared to compare the costs of in-house staff versus a low-bid contractor. (See Table 6-1.) While the figures clearly indicate that Wellesley should use in-house staff only, the reality is that both are used. The in-house staff handle routine trimming while the contractor is brought in for work on main streets, in the company of a police officer for traffic control, and for keeping to a routine pruning schedule when in-house crews fall behind. The contractor must also be available for emergencies such as ice or wind storms.

In other communities, the most commonly contracted services are tree removal and stump grinding. This is because specialized equipment is required and the equipment is not used often enough for the community to justify the expense of purchasing and maintaining the equipment. The other commonly contracted service is tree planting. This is chosen because the bulk of the work is done in the spring and sometimes the fall, when other park and tree service demands are at a peak and the labor force does not have time to plant trees.

There are several advantages to both contracted and in-house staff. Some advantages of contracted forestry work are as follows:

1. The cost is lower (depending on how costs are calculated).

2. Labor is available for peak work periods.

3. There is cancellation and thus no cost when work is not available, the weather is poor, equipment fails, or a crew

Table 6-1. Tree-Trimming Cost Comparison

Labor rate	Tree staff	Contractor	Notes
Foreman (25 percent time) (inspection)	$4.07	$4.07	1
Climber	13.01	20.50	
Laborer	10.78	20.20	
Retirement	9.75		2
Fringe benefit[3]	3.90	___	
	$41.51	44.77	

Equipment rate	Tree staff	Contractor	Notes
Foreman truck	$ 0.75	$0.75	
Aerial lift truck	12.25	26.25	
Chipper	6.00	3.00	
Accessory equipment	1.00		4
Depreciation	5.00	___	4
	$25.00	30.00	

The comparison indicates a total of $66.51 and $74.75. The comparison reflects 1990–1991 rates.

[1]The tree department foreman inspects both crews to ensure production and proper pruning, answer questions, and solve problems or respond to complaints.

[2]Thirty-five percent of the fringe benefit is for hospitalization and retirement. Tree company provides neither; it can be 100 percent paid by the employee.

[3]Fourteen percent of the fringe benefit is for sick time, vacation, etc. Tree company policy is: no work, no pay.

[4]Included in aerial truck rate.

member doesn't report for work.

4. Contractor provides employee supervision and training.

5. Contractors are specialists in trimming, planting, stump removal, etc., which makes them more efficient.

6. Work that does not meet quality standards, as specified, is not paid for.

7. City can easily switch to in-house staff if it wants a change.

8. Profit is greater.

9. It is ideal for scheduled trimming crews.

10. City can more easily effect a change of personnel.

Some advantages in the use of in-house staff are as follows:

1. The cost is lower (depending on how costs are calculated).

2. Staff is available for any and all facets of forestry operations.

3. No administrative time is necessary to write and oversee contracts.

4. Quality can be perfected to meet community standards through training.

5. In-house staff is more knowledgeable about the community.

6. In-house staffers respond quickly to emergencies.

7. The workforce is generally more stable.

8. Workers are motivated by pride and residency.

9. Use of in-house staff is ideal for demand pruning.

10. Cities find it more difficult to reduce budgets through layoffs.

Laws and Regulations

The laws and regulations which apply to an individual community will vary from state to state, community to community. It behooves every interested citizen and public supervisor to know what laws and regulations apply and to expand these laws in the interest of the community's environment.

The following example of state law has been taken from Massachusetts, while the zoning laws and subdivision rules are from Wellesley, Massachusetts. They have all been edited to make them more universally acceptable, and if used, they should be modified for each local community.

State Law

Massachusetts is typical of most states in having laws which give to local communities the right to request or establish a policy for obtaining and protecting street trees. An abridged version of this law begins below.

Section 1: Public Shade Trees Defined.   All trees within the boundaries of a public way shall be public shade trees.

Section 2: Powers of City Forester. The City Forester shall have the care and control of all public shade trees and shrubs in the municipality and shall enforce all the provisions of law for the preservation of such trees and shrubs. The City Forester shall expend all money appropriated for the setting out and maintenance of such trees. The City Forester may make regulations for the care and preservation of public shade trees and may establish fines.

Section 3: Cutting of Public Shade Trees. Hearing. Public shade trees shall not be cut, trimmed, or removed by any person other than the City Forester, even if he or she is the owner of property on which the tree is situated, except upon a permit in writing from the City Forester. Nor can trees be cut down or removed by the City Forester without a public hearing. The City Forester shall post a notice of the time and place of a hearing. The posting shall identify the size, type, and location of the shade tree or trees to be removed. The notice shall be posted at least 7 days before such hearing.

Section 4: Approval of Mayor Required If Objection Made. City Foresters shall not remove or grant a permit for the removal of a public shade tree if objection in writing is made by one or more persons, until removal or permit to remove is approved by the mayor.

Section 5: Cutting Down Bushes and Small Trees, Trimming Trees, etc., that Obstruct Travel. City Foresters may, without a hearing, trim or remove trees and bushes less than 1.5 inches in diameter, if ordered by the mayor or road commissioners, if the trees shall be deemed to obstruct or endanger persons traveling on the public way.

Section 6: Planting of Shade Trees. Cities and towns may appropriate money to the City Forester for planting shade trees in the public ways or upon adjoining land, at a distance not exceeding 20 feet from the public way, for the purpose of improving, protecting, shading, or ornamenting the public way, with the written consent of the landowner.

Section 7: Trees on State Highways. Only the Tree Department shall maintain and care for all trees and shrubs within the public way. Other persons may maintain public shade trees upon a permit in writing from the Tree Department.

Section 8: Signs and Marks on Shade Trees. Whoever affixes a sign, advertisement, or other thing to a tree in a public way, except for the purpose of protecting the tree or the public, shall be punished by a fine. City Foresters shall enforce the provisions of this section.

Section 9: Injury to Trees on State Highways. Whoever trims or removes a tree without authority within a state highway shall be punished by a fine.

Section 10: Injury to Trees of Another Person. Whoever willfully, maliciously, or wantonly cuts, destroys, or injures a tree, shrub, or growth which is not her or his own shall be punished by a fine.

Section 11: Injury to Shrubs, Trees, and Fixtures. Whoever wantonly injures, defaces, or destroys a shrub, plant, tree, fixture, ornament, or utility, in a public way, shall be punished by a fine and shall be liable in addition to the city or any person for all damages.

Local Zoning Ordinance

The local community with a zoning by-law can legally regulate, within state law guidelines, the amount of trees and landscaping, etc., that must be provided in parking lots and conservation districts. A Design Review Board can also regulate municipal landscaping.

Landscaping for Parking Lots. For an outdoor parking area containing twenty or more parking spaces, there shall be planted at least one tree for every ten parking spaces on any side of the perimeter of such parking area that abuts the sideline of a private or public way or abuts the lot line of land in residential districts or land used for residential purposes.

In any outdoor parking area, a landscaped open space having width of at least 5 feet and a depth equal to the adjacent parking space shall be provided so that there are no more than fifteen parking spaces in a continuous row. At least one tree shall be planted and maintained in each such open space.

However, where site plan approval is asking that relief be granted by this provision, an amount of landscaped open space equal in area to the provisions of this paragraph may be substituted, providing that such landscaped open space complies with the provisions of this section.

Trees required by the provisions of this section shall have a trunk of at least 2 inches in caliper, at the time of planting, and shall be of a species approved by the City Forester and by suitability and hardiness for location in a parking lot. To the extent practicable, existing trees shall be retained and used to satisfy the provisions of this section.

Conservation Districts.   In conservation districts, no new building or structure shall be constructed, used, or altered, and no land shall be used, for any purpose, except for conservation of soil, water, plants, and wildlife; outdoor recreation; dams and other water control devices; forestry; farming; nurseries; and gardening.

Design Review Board (DRB).   For the purposes of this example, the Design Review Board shall be appointed and shall consist of five city residents.

The Design Review Board shall review requests for Zoning Board special permits based on the following standards:

1. *Preservation and enhancement of landscaping.*   The landscape shall be preserved in its natural state, insofar as practicable, by minimizing tree and soil removal, and any grade changes shall be in keeping with the general appearance of neighboring developed areas.

2. *Relation of buildings to environment.*   Proposed development shall be related harmoniously to the terrain and to the use, scale, and architecture of existing buildings in the vicinity that have functional or visual relationship to the proposed buildings.

3. *Open space.*   All open space shall be designed to add to the visual amenities of the area.

4. *Signs and advertising devices.*   The size, location, design, color, texture, lighting, and materials of signs and advertising devices shall be in harmony with significant architectural features of existing and proposed buildings and structures and with surrounding properties.

5. *Heritage.*   Removal or disruption of historic, traditional, or significant uses, structures, or architectural elements shall be minimized insofar as practicable, whether these exist on the site or on adjacent properties.

Subdivision Rules and Regulations

If a community has regulations pertaining to subdivision development, they can establish the number of trees to be planted per lot in accordance with a master plan or the City Forester. The planting methods and species of trees can sometimes be regulated as well. An abridged example of these regulations follows:

Abridged Rules and Regulations Governing the Subdivision of Land.   In the section pertaining to subdivision design requirements, the following section can be included:

The developer shall plant or preserve at least one tree on each lot between the front line of the house and the street right-of-way.

Trees to be planted shall be at least 2.5 inches in trunk diameter. The species and variety of the trees to be planted shall be approved by the City Forester. Trees shall be planted in accordance with acceptable planting procedures.

Street Tree Ordinance

Every municipality and every municipal forestry or street tree department must operate under a set of rules and regulations. These policies will cover several areas, as described in the detailed examples which follow.

Street Tree Rules and Regulations

These rules regulate the performance of work on public shade trees as allowed by state law in order to protect the environment, provide protection to the shade trees, and preserve and enhance the natural beauty of the municipality.

Section 1: Sample Ordinance.   This ordinance shall be known as the Street Tree Ordinance for the city of (Name).

Section 2: Definitions.

City means the city of (Name).

Street tree means all trees within a public way or on the boundaries thereof which are public shade trees.

Urban Forester or *Arborist* means the person authorized to exercise the powers and authority granted by this ordinance.

Other definitions may apply to the local community.

Section 3: Street Tree Advocacy Committee. A group of citizens who have a special interest in municipal street tree care is established by this ordinance. This five-member board shall be appointed by the mayor for a term provided or until successors are appointed. At least three of the members should be trained in botany or a related field. The committee shall have the authority to elect officers, establish subcommittees, and adopt rules necessary for the management of the city's street trees.

The Citizens' Committee should be interested in all forms of tree care, tree celebration, and support for the tree maintenance programs. The committee can set up various celebrations such as Arbor Day; prepare articles for the local press; prepare guidelines for maintenance programs; participate in tree plantings; inform the public, neighborhood groups, school children, and other groups about the importance and care of trees; and prepare the street tree master plan.

Section 4: Urban Forester Duties. The Urban Forester is given the authority to manage all street trees within the city. The authority will be in accordance with regulations established in section 3. Management of the street trees shall consist of planting; maintaining; watering; pruning; treating disease and insect pests; and preserving, removing, and disposing of all street trees growing within the city.

The Urban Forester also has authority to maintain, at the homeowner's expense, any trees growing on private property that have become diseased or that endanger the public way and must be removed.

Section 5: Public Hearings. No public shade trees shall be cut down by the Urban Forester or any other person without a public hearing and without posting a notice upon the tree at least 7 days before such hearing.

Section 6: Permits. The Urban Forester shall issue permits for management of public street trees.

1. No person shall plant, prune, remove, or endanger the health of a public shade tree before obtaining a permit from the Urban Forester.

2. No person shall excavate or do any other potentially damaging work within a radius of 10 feet from the trunk of a public shade tree without first obtaining a written permit from the Urban Forester.

3. Application for permits must be made with the Urban Forester

no less than 48 hours in advance of when the work is to be done.

4. Permits shall be issued only if the proposed work will not injure the tree or its roots.

5. Permits pertaining to tree care shall be issued only to certified arborists or private citizens and contractors who are qualified to perform the work.

6. Permits must be kept on the job site during the progress of the work and must be shown upon request to the Urban Forester's staff and police officers.

7. Before a permit is issued for work under these regulations, the applicant shall provide insurance as required for work in public ways.

8. All work on public shade trees shall be completed under the direction of the Urban Forester in a good workmanlike manner by using standard arboricultural practices and methods. The general public, public and private property, and vegetation in the work area shall be protected during the work period.

9. No person shall affix to any public shade tree any notice or sign or shall cut or paint anything without a permit issued by the Urban Forester.

10. The Urban Forester may at any time cancel, revoke, or modify permits for a cause such as the cancellation of insurance.

11. Any person who removes a public shade tree without a permit shall be subject to a fine of up to $500. Such fines shall be in addition to fines provided for in these regulations.

Section 7: Fines.   The following fines are established for each separate violation of these rules and regulations.

Cutting or marking a tree in any way	$_____
Attaching a sign to a tree without a permit	_____
Injuring or removing the bark of a tree	_____
Driving any object into a tree	_____
Injuring or cutting the roots of a tree	_____
Continuing work after suspension or revocation of a permit	_____
Placement of anything at or near a tree that damages it in any way	_____

A separate violation shall be deemed to have been committed for each day following notification to cease the violation, and additional fines shall be assessed for each day.

Section 8: Enforcement. The Urban Forester shall enforce all laws enacted for the protection of public shade trees and shall seek complaints in appropriate courts of law for violations of such laws.

Any order issued by the Urban Forester shall have a time limit for compliance. In case of extreme danger or hazard, the order can be effective immediately.

The order can be appealed to the mayor provided that it is filed within 5 days. If the order is not completed, the Urban Forester can take steps to solve the problem. The Urban Forester can file a special assessment against the property upon which the hazard exists. The assessment will cover the cost to remedy the situation.

Section 9: Street Tree Planting. This section is adopted in order to enhance the beauty of the community and the health and welfare of its citizens as well as to replace the declining population of street trees.

The Urban Forester or the budget-controlling board will determine the number of street trees to be planted annually. The species of tree will be selected by the Urban Forester and the landowner in accordance with the Street Tree Master Plan (or the list which follows). Only one to two trees per lot will by planted by the Tree Department. Undesirable trees (see list) should not be planted on city property or public streets unless specifically approved by the Urban Forester. These lists may be revised periodically.

Trees will be planted to replace recently removed trees or upon request of a landowner. When trees are planted on private land, the written consent of the landowner is required (see the example which follows). The landowner must also agree in writing to maintain and care for the tree after it is planted. Trees planted with public funds on private land are then the responsibility of the landowner and/or lessee. (This provision may be changed to abide by local laws and policies.)

NAME _____DATE PLANTED _____
ADDRESS _____ NUMBER OF TREES _____
NAME OF TREE(S) _____

I hereby grant permission to (Name of community or tree department) to plant above named trees on my land under the provisions of (Local or state law).

These trees are public shade trees, and if deemed necessary, the Tree Department may enter this property at any time to spray, trim, or remove these trees, but is under no obligation to do so.

SIGNATURE OF PROPERTY OWNER _____

The Urban Forester will determine the best locations and species for planting trees in cooperation with the landowner. Trees will be planted where they can provide a benefit and within the following distance requirements:

Distance from:	Minimum, feet	Maximum, feet	Preferred, feet
Utilities—underground	10	40	20
Utilities—overhead—small trees only	10	40	25
Hydrant, utility poles, and light posts	10	30	15
Street line	8	20	12
Intersection	20	50	30
Driveway			
Small tree	5	20	15
Large tree	15	30	20
Other trees and buildings			
Small trees	20	60	30
Medium trees	30	80	40
Large trees	40	100	50

A standard procedure for tree planting shall be established by the Urban Forester.

Planting stock specifications will be reviewed periodically by the Urban Forester. Unless indicated otherwise, all public street trees shall conform to the American Association of Nurserymen Standards. Bare-root trees shall be at least 1.25 to 1.5 inches in diameter and balled-and-burlapped trees shall be at least 2 to 2.5 inches in diameter, measured 6 inches aboveground.

All trees shall have straight trunks and be well branched. There shall be no disease or injury apparent. The roots and top shall be well developed and characteristic of the species.

Planting procedures should follow current accepted arboricultural standards. Once the tree is planted, all other maintenance except pruning and removal will be controlled by the Street Tree Master Plan and the professional judgment of the Urban Forester.

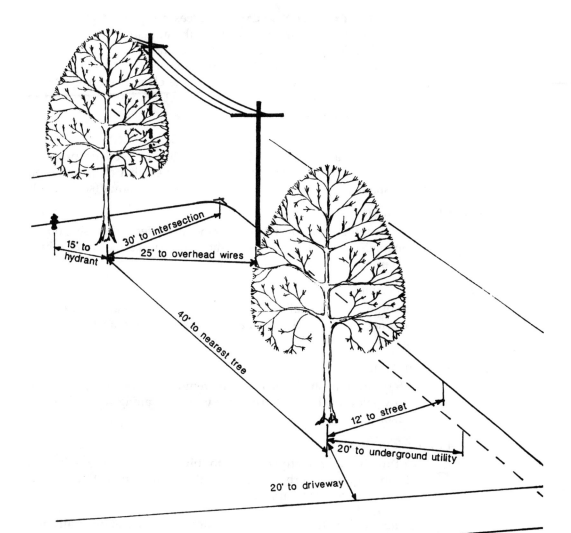

Minimum distances for tree planting.

Section 10: Pruning Standards. Trees are pruned to preserve their health and appearance and to make adjustments which will increase their longevity in an urban environment.

Pruning will reduce or eliminate hazards to human life and public property and can provide adequate clearance for electrical conductors. A minimum height of 6 feet above the ground is sufficient for sidewalk clearance.

Types of Pruning

In 1988 the National Arborist Association revised its pruning standards. The Urban Forester has determined that all pruning on public shade trees shall be class ―――― defined as follows (select one):

Class 1 Fine Pruning

Fine pruning shall consist of the removal of dead, diseased, objectionable, and weak branches on the main trunks and limbs which are larger than $\frac{1}{2}$ inch in diameter.

Class 2 Medium Pruning

Medium pruning shall consist of the removal of dead, diseased, objectionable, and weak branches which are larger than 1 inch in diameter.

Class 3 Safety Pruning

Safety pruning shall consist of the removal of the dead, diseased, and weak branches that are a size which in falling would injure a person.

Class 4 Cutback to Topping

Cutting back, drop crotching, or topping consists of the reduction of tops, sides, underbranches, or individual limbs with attention given to a symmetric appearance.

(When a class for street trees is chosen, class 1 is generally too expensive for most municipalities and class 4 is not acceptable arboricultural practice.)

Section 11: Tree Removal. To determine a uniform procedure, this tree removal section has been prepared. Although the reasons are varied, decisions to remove trees will be made by the highest elected officials of the community in order to protect the public safety and welfare, to preserve the environment, and to protect the harmonious setting of the community and its trees.

Candidates for removal are those trees which are dead, diseased, or life-endangering. Other trees may be removed upon the proper

Tree Selection—the B&B soil must be similar to the planting site. Select a tree suited to the site based upon mature size, acceptable species or variety and nursery grown.

Planting Season—B.R. trees in spring. B&B or container trees any time the soil is workable, March 15 to Oct. 15, provided the tree was dug in the spring prior to bud break.

Only plant trees with hard root balls.

Prune only broken, diseased, dead or poor branches and roots.

Always remove rope, wire, plastic, artificial and green burlap at planting time.

Bare Root trees larger than 3˝ and trees that have dried out are not acceptable.

Container grown trees cannot exceed 2˝ diameter. Any roots encircling the container must be cut or extended out into the backfill.

Watering must be done when the roots are half covered, immediately after planting is completed, and twice during the next 24 hours. Thereafter, the tree must be watered thoroughly once a week until the end of the growing season.

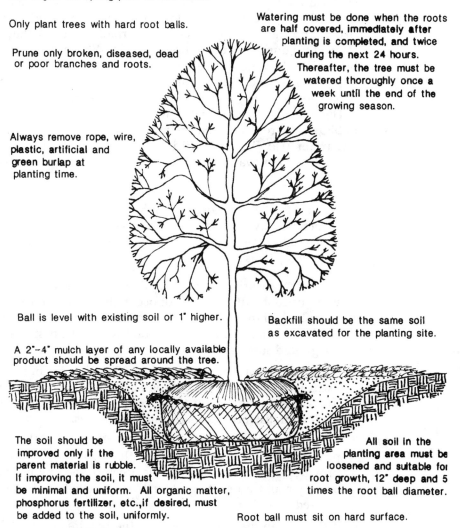

Ball is level with existing soil or 1˝ higher.

A 2˝–4˝ mulch layer of any locally available product should be spread around the tree.

Backfill should be the same soil as excavated for the planting site.

The soil should be improved only if the parent material is rubble. If improving the soil, it must be minimal and uniform. All organic matter, phosphorus fertilizer, etc.,if desired, must be added to the soil, uniformly.

All soil in the planting area must be loosened and suitable for root growth, 12˝ deep and 5 times the root ball diameter.

Root ball must sit on hard surface.

Tree planting detail and specification.

conduct of a public hearing in accordance with these rules and regulations.

Storm-damaged trees shall be restored and made safe according to the following priorities: (1) Remove immediate life hazards. (2) If within the department's jurisdiction, remove trees and branches from electric lines to enable line workers to restore electric service. (3) Clear all trees and limbs obstructing roadways. (4) Remove large trees which present a hazard to private property or other trees. (5) Brush and debris will be left at the roadside until they can be cleaned up during regular working hours. Whenever streets will be blocked off because of tree removal operations, the police and fire departments need notification. These departments need to know where, for how long, and when the street is reopened.

The Tree Department may, without a hearing, cut or remove public shade trees less than 1.5 inches in diameter which obstruct or endanger travelers or buildings. Nothing shall prevent the trimming or removal of any tree which endangers persons traveling on a highway.

Section 12: Root Pruning.   Whenever any and all types of construction activity, being performed within or in close proximity to public rights-of-way and easements, come within 10 feet of a tree, the following items apply:

1. For trees measuring 12 inches in diameter or less, soil excavation work or root cutting shall not occur closer than 3 feet from the outer bark of the tree. For multistemmed trees, the measurement shall be taken at the narrowest point within the first 2 feet above the ground surface.

2. For trees measuring greater than 12 inches in diameter, soil excavation work or root cutting shall not occur closer than the distance measured by the circumference of the tree or a maximum distance of 6 feet, whichever is less.

3. Soil excavation work may be done closer than the distance parameters established under the above two categories, provided all excavation of soil is accomplished by hand shovel or auger and no roots greater than 2 inches in diameter are severed.

4. If there is an inability to perform the requirements established under the aforementioned three situations, a representative from the municipal forestry department shall be called to the tree site to make an inspection and recommendation pertaining to the need to remove the tree. Unless other provisions are specified, trees removed by the city will be removed and replaced at cost to

the contractor or department authorizing the construction. The replacement tree(s) will be in accordance with section 13 of these regulations.

5. If removal of the tree is required by private and public utilities, contractors, and others under life-threatening or related emergency situations, removal of the tree(s) is authorized without written authorization, providing that proper follow-up written documentation is done and a replacement is given the forestry department as soon as possible.

6. For new construction involving noncity projects, the initiating agency shall replace each tree removed as determined by section 13 of these regulations. The term *new construction* is defined as a facility that does not presently exist in the same property area as the proposed construction. Any tree removed that is determined by the forestry department to be dead or dying will not be considered as lost value.

Section 13: Unauthorized Tree Removal. Occasionally public trees are removed by people without permission. When this occurs, the trees can be protected and replaced with a "replacement policy." This section is also concerned with the replacement of public trees removed or damaged by construction activities.

Any person, firm, corporation, or agency that in the course of construction intends to remove any tree 2.5 inches or greater in caliper within the jurisdiction of the municipal forestry department shall post a bond with the department. This bond ensures that within 30 days after the completion of construction all trees removed or severely damaged shall be replaced on a caliper inch-for-inch basis at the expense of the person, firm, corporation, or agency.

Location, species, and caliper of replacement trees shall be determined in consultation with the municipal forestry department in keeping with the Street Tree Master Plan. The total caliper of all replacement trees planted shall equal or exceed the total caliper of all trees severely damaged or removed.

Replacement trees shall be balled and burlapped and not less than 2.5-inch caliper. Planting shall be in keeping with usual and customary arboricultural standards and shall take place in spring or fall, as determined by the municipal forestry department.

The amount of the bond shall be determined by the Urban Forester and shall be sufficient to cover the cost of replacement. The bond shall be held for 1 year from the date of planting to ensure survival of the replacement tree(s).

Tree Preservation Ordinance

Tree preservation ordinances have been developed to protect trees on private property. According to statistics generated by ACRT, 14 percent of 946 cities surveyed in the United States have tree preservation ordinances. These ordinances are particularly useful in cities that are rapidly growing and where at least several subdivisions per year are being built. The purpose of these ordinances is to

1. Ensure a given percentage of forest in new development projects
2. Prevent clear-cutting of blocks of land that is useful for buffer, screening, or view enhancement
3. Control runoff, soil erosion, and drainage problems onto abutting land
4. Minimize temperature elevation, decrease air pollution, and lower carbon dioxide levels on land that could become defoliated by development
5. Protect and enhance the aesthetic values of a city on developable sites
6. Enhance the value of the land and all its trees
7. Educate developers as to the value of trees and how to protect and preserve them during construction
8. Protect trees and define the permits, fees, penalties, and other legal requirements necessary to preserve the forest

Sample Tree Ordinance

The following sample tree ordinance has been edited to serve as an amendment to a municipality zoning by-law or ordinance. This sample is one of the best in the United States and was originally written for Fulton County, Georgia; it has been edited to make it more universally acceptable.

1. Intent.   It is the intent of these regulations to provide standards for the preservation of trees as part of the land development and building construction process for the purpose of making (City name) (hereafter called the City), a more attractive place to live, to provide a healthy living environment, and to better maintain control of flooding, noise, glare and soil erosion.

2. Benefit of Trees.   Trees provide beneficial oxygen while reducing the levels of harmful carbon dioxide. They reduce air pollution, purify water, and stabilize the soil. Trees provide wildlife habitat and shade, cool the land, reduce noise, and provide an aesthetic value to the land.

The protection of trees throughout this City is vital to the survival of our residents, and protection is necessary for every tree in the City.

3. Definitions

(a) *Buildable area:* The portion of a lot which is not located within any minimum required yard, landscape area, or buffer, i.e., that portion of a lot wherein a building may be located.

(b) *City:* The City known as (Name).

(c) *Land disturbance permit (development permit):* A permit issued by the City that authorizes the commencement of development on a given tract of land.

(d) *Landscape plan:* A plan that identifies areas of tree preservation and methods of tree protection within the protected zone as well as all areas of replanting. Within replanting areas, the common and botanical names of the proposed species, the number of plants of each species, the size of all plant materials, the proposed location of all plant materials, and any unique features of the plant materials shall be indicated.

(e) *Municipal arborist:* The agent of the City having primary enforcement responsibilities under this ordinance and charged with the responsibility for approval of all landscape plans for land development in the City required pursuant to this ordinance.

(f) *Protected zone:* All lands that fall outside the buildable area of a parcel, all areas of the parcel required to remain an open space, and all areas required as landscaping strips according to provisions of the City zoning regulations or conditions of zoning approval.

(g) *Protected tree:* Any tree which has been determined by the municipal arborist to be of high value because of its type, size, age, or other professional criteria and which has been so designated.

(h) *Tree:* Any self-supporting woody perennial plant which has a trunk diameter of 2 inches or more, measured at a point 6 inches above the ground level, and which normally obtains a height of at least 10 feet at maturity.

(i) *Zoning regulations:* The City's Zoning Resolution as amended or such other regulations subsequently adopted by the City Council, inclusive of conditions of zoning approval established pursuant thereto.

(j) *All other terms:* All other words or phrases as appropriate to the context of their uses shall be interpreted as defined in the Zoning Regulations.

4. Applicability.   The terms and provisions of this ordinance shall apply to any activity on real property which requires the issuance of Land Disturbance Permit wetlands protection permit, building permit, or subdivision permit within the City, but excluding the construction of individual, single-family, detached and duplex dwellings. No Land Disturbance Permit shall be issued by the City without it being determined that the proposed development is in conformance with the provisions of these regulations.

5. Permit Procedure

(a) All applications for a Land Disturbance Permit shall provide a landscaping plan and other documentation as required below (and applicable) for all areas of the parcel within a protected zone.

(b) All plans should contain the following information: shape and dimensions of the lot and proposed structures; precise location of all trees correctly identified; trees to remain, to be transplanted, and to be removed; procedures or techniques for the protection of existing trees during construction; location of setbacks according to section 6c; and proposed grade changes.

(c) All landscape plans and related documentation shall be reviewed by the municipal arborist for conformance to the provisions of these regulations and approved, returned for revisions, or denied within 30 days of receipt. If denied, the reasons for denial shall be annotated on the landscape plan or otherwise stated in writing.

(d) Issuance of the Land Disturbance Permit shall constitute approval of the required landscape plan and conformance to the provisions of these regulations.

(e) Fees to cover the administration costs may be charged.

6. Removal of Trees and Replacement Landscaping

(a) Trees are not to be removed in the protected zone unless the owner and/or developer documents an economic hardship if the trees in the protected zone were preserved. Said documentation shall be submitted as part of the application for a Land Disturbance Permit. Diseased or damaged trees and trees that pose a safety hazard to pedestrians, vehicles, buildings, or utilities or that block access to the site may be removed. Nothing in these regulations shall be construed to allow the removal of vegetation in a natural, undisturbed buffer required by zoning regulations.

(b) When no trees are present in the protected zone, or the existing trees are unhealthy and not worth saving, or when it is proposed that any portion of the protected zone be disturbed, it shall be the responsibility of the owner and/or developer to landscape said areas (where improvements are not constructed) with trees or other plant materials subject to zoning regulations or, in lieu thereof, administrative standards established by the City.

(c) When grading is to occur outside of the buildable area on a parcel or when the buildable area leaves no protected zone adjacent to a property line, the minimum following landscape areas shall be established along peripheral property lines unless zoning regulations require more: Front, 40 feet; side on corner, 40 feet; side—interior, 10 feet; rear, 10 feet.

Said landscape areas shall be landscaped pursuant to zoning regulations or, in lieu thereof, administrative standards established by the City.

(d) Not withstanding any of the other requirements of these regulations, it shall be unlawful to remove a specimen tree without the express written permission of the Municipal Arborist. Administrative standards may be established by the City for the identification, preservation, and protection of specimen trees.

(e) This regulation does not apply to trees less than 2 inches in diameter, hazardous species as defined by the Municipal Arborist, government employees operating in a declared emergency, nurseries, and tree farms.

(f) Prior to removal, all trees must be flagged, and the clearing areas must be identified for field inspection.

(g) A "tree bank" may be set up by the City to receive any trees that may be desirable but have to be removed from the disturbed areas. These trees will be dug and replanted at the City's expense within 30 days of the date of the approved plan.

7. Enforcement. It shall be the duty of the Municipal Arborist to enforce this ordinance. The Arborist shall have the authority to revoke, suspend, or void the Land Disturbance Permit and shall have the authority to suspend all work on a site or any portion thereof.

8. Violation and Penalty.   Any person, firm, or corporation violating any of the provisions of this ordinance shall be deemed guilty of a misdemeanor. Each day's continuance of a violation and each tree removed shall be considered a separate offense. The owner of any property wherein a violation exists—and any builder, contractor, or agent who may have assisted in the commission of any such violation—shall be guilty of a separate offense.

9. Appeal

(a) Any person aggrieved or affected by any decision of the Municipal Arborist relating to the application of these regulations may appeal to the City for relief or reconsideration. Any person aggrieved or affected by any decision of the City relating to the application of these regulations may file an appeal within 30 days of the decision.

(b) Appeals shall be granted only for errors of interpretation, or where the unique natural features of the site are such that application of these regulations would create an undue hardship to the property owner, or in instances where an undue hardship is created for the owner of the property.

Sources

ACRT: *Vancouver Street Tree Plan*, Kent, OH, 1990.
ACRT: *Street Tree Inventory and Management Plan for Huntsville, Alabama*, Kent, OH, 1989.
City of Toledo, Ohio, "Construction near Street Trees Policy," 1991.
Massachusetts General Laws, *MGL Chapter 87, Shade Trees*, Boston, as amended.
Miller, Robert W.: *Urban Forestry, Planning and Managing Urban Greenspaces*, Prentice-Hall, Englewood Cliffs, NJ, 1988.
Phillips, L. E.: "Unionized Tree Climbers," *City Trees*, May/June 1989, p. 5.
Phillips, L. E.: "Incapacitated Employees," *City Trees*, December 1986, p. 14.
Phillips, L. E.: "Wellesley Street Tree Master Plan," Town of Wellesley, MA, 1979.
Stankovich, Michael K.: "A Master Plan for Street Tree Planting," City of Oak Park, IL, 1984.
Wellesley (MA) Planning Board, Zoning By-Law, 1977, as amended.

Endnote

Catalogs from Karl Kuemmerling, American Arborist Supplies, Aerial Lift, Asplundh, and Vermeer.

7

Public Relations Programs

Public relations programs are necessary to keep park or forestry programs intact. The purpose of public relations efforts is also to inform residents about trees, the role of trees in the environment, and what is necessary to care for them. The ideas in this chapter help preserve the public's perception that a department is on top.

Volunteers

Although most communities have full-time tree care staff capable of maintaining street trees, other activities which require lots of time, effort, and people also require demands often beyond the capabilities of the staff. Getting these projects implemented can be accomplished by using volunteers while paid staff concentrate on more pressing demands.

The most important volunteers are those who serve on the tree advisory board for your community. This board guides and promotes the urban forest management. This citizens' committee should be interested in all forms of tree care, tree celebrations, and support for the tree maintenance programs. The committee can set up various celebrations such as Arbor Day; prepare articles for the local press; prepare guidelines for maintenance programs; participate in tree plantings; conduct special pruning projects; inform the public, neighborhood groups, school children, and other groups about the importance and care of trees; conduct the street tree inventory; and prepare the street tree master plan.

The major disadvantage in using volunteers is the inability and unwillingness of some cities to insure volunteers against injury. Most states have already settled this issue by indicating that anyone who does work for another is covered by that employer's workers' compensation plan. However, since many cities are self-insured, they have chosen not to include volunteers as employees.

Experience has proved, however, that volunteers actually have better safety records than paid employees. The reasons are threefold: (1) Volunteers work without time limitations and pressure to get the job done; so while the work may take longer, there is less carelessness, and fewer shortcuts, which cause accidents, are taken. (2) Volunteers are seldom given the opportunity to use heavy or dangerous equipment. (3) Volunteers are volunteering because they want to do a municipal project without costing taxpayers, like themselves. Using this same philosophy, volunteers who get injured will usually go to their own physician rather than file a claim against the city, which in turn might burden the taxpayer. Volunteer supervision will prevent any claim of gross negligence.

Therefore, the workers' compensation issue does not pose an obstacle to the use of volunteers. However, labor unions have traditionally opposed the use of volunteers, who are seen as taking work and overtime away from dues-paying members. Successful volunteer programs have been able to avoid union problems by one of two methods: (1) Before establishing a volunteer program, meet with union officials and get their endorsement for the program. Once the union has approved, with or without conditions and limitations, the program can grow rapidly and without opposition. (2) Use volunteers to cover projects formerly done by union labor or not being done with union labor. Most employees will recognize that the volunteers are helping them do their job and that without the volunteers' help, the job would not be done. Then this would be a poor reflection on union members. This approach runs the risk of union opposition at any time, with or without cause and usually with ensuing poor publicity.

When properly utilized, volunteers can be a valuable resource. A successful volunteer program requires the development of a plan that uses volunteers to their best advantage and a central program coordinator who will encourage more volunteers to participate. The coordinator should organize the program and then provide training, recognition, supervision, and evaluation of the volunteers.

The Volunteer Program

Volunteer programs will not reduce the budget unless volunteers displace paid staff. Volunteers offer the capacity to make more productive application of existing funds and personnel, enabling staff to increase the level and quality of services delivered.

Seeking volunteers is not the first step. The first priority is the establishment of a set of goals and objectives, such as developing a street tree inventory or street tree master plan. Then a determination should be made as to the time and task requirements. Goals which are 3 years away might be unrealistic and discouraging to the volunteer, but goals 6 months apart provide a desirable incentive. Be advised that while there are many advantages to using volunteers, the major disadvantage will be the very slow rate of progress. Have a plan, and it will be done.

The volunteer program should be organized to respond to the motivations of volunteers and should be linked to the structure of the agency. Management of a volunteer program is a job in itself, which requires time, planning, education, and training.

The components of a good volunteer program are the following: record keeping, job description, recruitment, interviewing, placement, orientation, training, supervision, dealing with staff, motivation, recognition, retention, and evaluation.

Record Keeping

A system must be set up to organize the records of the entire volunteer program. The records should keep track of the volunteers, jobs, retention efforts, and service and training records of volunteers. The records are needed to document legal responsibilities, for accountability, and for evaluations. However, the records should be considered confidential.

Job Description

The volunteer needs a description of the tasks expected. When volunteers are working in parks, for example, the duties might consist of weeding, mowing, flower care, pruning, trash cleanup, etc. For volunteers working on forestry, functions might be more difficult to define. However, the job description, where duties are evident, can include items such as a job title, working hours or time requirements, goals, training, responsibilities, qualifications, benefits, and supervision. Job descriptions are also useful for publicizing volunteer activities while at the same time creating a clear distinction between the volunteer and paid staff job descriptions. The job description can be used to define the value of the volunteer labor. This monetary value can justify the entire volunteer program.

Recruitment

A recruitment program should attract potential volunteers from the entire community. Efforts to seek volunteers include the use of radio and newspaper articles and advertisements, municipal brochures and public announcements, and word of mouth. Once a potential volunteer has come forward, an application will be useful in defining the training, skills, and background of the volunteer. This information can be used to match the applicant to the job. Often the volunteer might have her or his own ideas about a specific area or function to adopt. In these cases, the formal job description and placement efforts need to be modified.

Recruitment efforts should also be directed to obtain volunteers with appropriate backgrounds for the jobs available. With the increasing demand for and a limited supply of volunteers, the recruitment process becomes very challenging.

Volunteer programs should also consider groups of volunteers. These groups can come from civic organizations, garden clubs, boy and girl scouts of all ages, businesses and contractors, landscape maintenance and tree care companies, and local nurseries and garden centers. Don't forget to accept donations in lieu of volunteers, when contacting these various groups.

Interview

Once a potential volunteer applicant has applied, she or he should be interviewed. The interview will clarify the expectations of the volunteer and enable the municipality to carefully screen and select volunteers. The interview will determine how desires, skills, and capabilities of the volunteers relate to the needs of the municipality.

Placement

Volunteers need to be very carefully matched to the tasks available. This will meet the needs of both the volunteer and the municipality. Follow-up and supervision are also required to ensure compatibility between the task and the volunteer. Careful planning is essential so the volunteer has a reasonable project, all the necessary tools, a timetable, and the necessary training required for success.

Project assignments should be made so that volunteers remain interested, enthusiastic, and proud of their assignments.

Orientation and Training

Volunteers need an orientation on the first day to find out their duties and responsibilities. Since volunteers often lack experience in working with government, orientation will familiarize them with operations, procedures, and employees. Volunteers may not want to follow the rules, and since social interaction is part of the fun of volunteering, managers have to respect this attitude.

Training makes a volunteer knowledgeable and skilled. The training program consists of orientation followed by an overview of the municipal operations and then a study of details in the project area. In-service training will show the volunteers how to put theory into practice. Training will teach them the skills they will need to meet the requirements of the job description.

Supervision

Clear lines of communication and supervision are essential in volunteer programs. Volunteers need to know who to talk with so that paid staffers are not offended and the volunteers are not misdirected. This effort clarifies the line of authority and facilitates accountability. Supervision of volunteers is best handled by a volunteer services director, who communicates directly with paid staff through the chain of command.

Motivation and Recognition

Volunteer recognition ceremonies and other incentives are a modest form of appreciation. Some communities that have successful volunteer programs have the most success with a volunteers' picnic. At this event, the volunteers meet each other and the paid staff as well. They all applaud the awarding of certificates, and the event is very inexpensive. Some major cities offer incentives to volunteers such as free gate admissions, free admissions for guests, special classes, early admission to special events, and other incentives as varied as the communities which have volunteers. Recognition incentives can include a suggestion box; reimbursement for expenses; attention to personal needs and problems; awards of simple things such as certificates, flowers, bulbs or plants, photographs, and other small tokens of appreciation; recognition by the local press; taking time to talk; sending holiday cards; saying thank you; and a smile. Photographs of the volunteer at work, with copies sent to the local press, rewards the volunteer and encourages others to participate. Above all, volunteers need a positive image to identify with. Also consider events for the volunteers such as seminars, walks, or tours with nature and environmental themes.

Evaluation and Retention

An evaluation of the whole volunteer program is as important as an evaluation of the individual volunteers. The evaluations should relate to attainment of the stated goals as well as the needs, growth, and satisfaction of the volunteer.

The evaluation of the volunteer program should begin with a survey completed by the volunteers to evaluate the training program, the usefulness and pros and cons of the program, and the assignments. The program should also be analyzed to determine its cost-effectiveness. Thus the dollar value of donated labor is compared to the administrative and expense costs.

Employee evaluation is a difficult task for municipal employers because of their reluctance to challenge well-meaning efforts. However, evaluations do guide the volunteer toward improvement in achieving worthwhile and visible results. Allowing inappropriate behavior, mistakes, or faulty assignments to continue without comment is an insult to the volunteer. A positive evaluation might encourage volunteer renewal as well as expansion of volunteer efforts.

Tasks

Volunteers can perform a wide range of tasks to assist the staff of a forestry department. Volunteers can prune, water, and plant new trees. They can also be used, with extra training, to assist in the taking of an inventory. They can plan where future trees should be planted. Communities with a municipality-owned forest can send volunteer crews into the area to manage the trees with selected removals and careful pruning.

Volunteers are especially helpful in running Arbor Day celebrations or public relations campaigns with speakers lists and slide shows. They can give tours, do research, and perform other miscellaneous tasks. They can be used for special projects when a large number of people are necessary to handle special events. Examples include preparing seedlings for Arbor Day distribution, potting plants for a spring sale, and special events in the parks or recreation programs. Some cities have developed programs employing volunteers to prune small trees and newly planted trees. These programs require a special training session and a pole pruner to reach the tips of these small trees. The volunteers prune only those trees that can be pruned from the ground and with the pole pruner. Most park departments have enormous labor requirements that volunteers can help meet.

Smaller cities can develop volunteer programs to assist with very specific programs such as Adopt-a-Park or Traffic Island. These programs, by their nature, can get by with a less sophisticated volunteer program more easily than those mentioned above. Record keeping, placement, orientation, training, supervision, motivation, recognition, and retention are important tasks even in small programs as informal as those having only one or two volunteers.

Remember that one enthusiastic volunteer can assemble an entire committee just through word of mouth. A volunteer's pride will increase his or her desire to complete the initial assignment and then encourage others to volunteer as well.

Ideas

Listed below are many ideas that can be used to promote better relations between a forestry department and local residents.

Open House.   This event can show off the equipment, current projects, and beautification programs. Free seedlings or flowers can be passed out. Staff should be available to answer questions and discuss tree maintenance concerns and current pest problems. Have pamphlets that have been purchased or made locally, concerning tree care, local parks, etc., available for free distribution. Mount large photographs on display boards to capture the public's attention, and then have text available for those interested in learning more about what the photographs illustrate.

Public Displays.   In addition to slide shows, public displays are sent to the library and city hall whenever special projects or events warrant the attention or will draw a crowd.

Arbor Day Program.   This provides an opportunity for tree planting programs to stress tree management and distribute tree care booklets. Use politicians, pass out seedlings, and have children participate for best results.

Tree City—USA.   This is a high-interest program that can be continued year after year. Use the Tree City—USA sign at entrances to the city, fly the flag in the center of the city, and use the logo on forestry stationery.

Local Press.   The press should be used for news releases that indicate who, what, where, when, and why. Call the local reporters in

Photographs and master plans displayed at a recycling facility.

advance of an event. If something bad happens, call back with prepared comments.

Newsletters.   Some cities mail a newsletter covering local government news to every resident. The forestry department should prepare an article for every issue. This medium is especially effective for timely subjects such as spray programs, seasonal diseases, etc.

Cable TV.   This medium should be used as much as the local newspaper. Take advantage of the small viewing audience to practice in front of the camera. If a major event occurs that brings in the network news, the forestry department spokesperson is then prepared and relaxed with the press.

Summary of the Street Tree Master Plan.   A summary is a useful tool to give the public and political leaders as an explanation to the value of the plan. The information contained in the plan can also be analyzed by the public with feedback regarding the opinions and levels of support for the tree management program. This summary can explain how the community can obtain the highest-quality urban forestry program for the funds available.

Tree City—USA flag flies under the U.S. flag.

Billboards.   These are used by some communities to promote urban forestry programs. However, many environmentalists feel this program is counterproductive since billboards tend to "litter" the landscape aesthetically.

Adopt-a-Tree.   Many communities use this program to increase public awareness of trees. This designation of a "city tree" is made through suggestions, public opinion, survey, or election by the local tree advisory committee. The photograph clearly indicates the favorite tree of Westerville, Ohio.

Mascots.   Several communities use urban forestry mascots to help promote their programs and to teach people—children especially—all about conservation principles. Examples include Smoky the Bear, who represents forest fire prevention; Elmer the Elm, who talks about trees, Woodsy Owl, who supports litter cleanup and the slogan "Give a Hoot, Don't Pollute"; and Spunky Squirrel, whose slogan is "Plan, Plant, Preserve, and Protect."

Resident Inquiries.   Inquiries should be answered by phone, by

Routed post at City Hall illustrates Westerville, Ohio's "city tree." (*Photo courtesy Richard Rano.*)

letter, or in person. Respond promptly, factually, and courteously. Keep note of your appearance, tone of voice, and choice of words; listen carefully to the questions and answer them concisely.

Brochures and Displays.   These should look as professional as possible and be complete but to the point. Subjects should be timely and should address concerns of the residents.

Door Hangers or Door Knob Cards.   These are popular for tree trimming notifications which prevent complaints before trimming occurs. Other door hanging brochures that highlight tree planting or special diseases or pests in the neighborhood are very popular.

Office Secretaries.   These workers should have excellent telephone manners because they provide the first impressions. The secretary should also be informed of work crew and staff activities.

Local Parades.   Parade officials usually call the Department of Public Works to assist in setting up staging, closing streets, etc., for local parades. Why not spend one day of labor to decorate an excellent-looking flat-bed truck with a banner, shrubs, flowers, sod, and mulch and join in the parade with a float? (A photograph of one example is shown on page 165.)

Plant Flowers.   At major intersections or in heavily used parks, plant flowers. Make sure the flowers receive the best care available whether from volunteers, contractors, or city labor. Flowers also draw attention to maintenance efforts. Even if the maintenance has been going on for years, it is never noticed until it stops or until flowers are planted.

Traffic Islands.   These are usually paved over. Develop a program to convert pavement to low-maintenance trees, shrubs, or flowers. Grass requires weekly mowing while heavily mulched shrubs, ground covers, or low-maintenance perennials can be visited once a month for a quick weeding.

Equipment.   Equipment should be kept clean, waxed, and (if funds are available) repainted when necessary. Beautiful equipment displays pride, and pride is transferred to the operations and the public's perception of the department. Uniforms for the employees also reinforce this attitude.

Wellesley, Massachusetts, Park and Tree division fleet and employees in 1988 Park Centennial uniforms.

Routine Tree Care.   A 3- to 5-year cycle is good for routine tree care. The more often the work is done, the smaller the branches that have to be removed and the fewer complaints that will be received. The work goes faster as well, and storm damage is minimized because the trees are in better condition.

New Projects.   Encourage new projects. The willingness to take on additional responsibilities (with appropriate funding) creates a positive attitude from the public who have a perception that the answer is always no! It also emphasizes your importance, value, labor skills, and diversity. And employees like the change of pace.

Creative Funding.   This should be everyone's goal. Have the electric company pay the tree crews to do line trimming in the city. Use parking meter receipts to pay for public parking lot landscaping. Garden clubs and civic organizations will often support special beautification projects. Encourage local neighborhoods and individuals to adopt a park, to support care, and to raise funds for their projects. Collect from insurance companies for any vehicular damage to trees or public property. Sell trees, planted and watered at the retail price, to homeowners. (When trees are purchased at

Top: Equipment is Mack truck, photographed when 7 years old. *Bottom:* Local parade in Wellesley, Massachusetts, in 1988. Sod, bricks, and flowers are all planted in mulch on top of flatbed truck to make a float. Materials were used later in Wellesley parks. Preparation took 1 day and a crew of three to clean the truck and install the decorations.

Plant flowers in town square (*top left*), at base of tree near a duck pond (*top right*), and in London Plane tree planter in center of town (*bottom*).

Landscaped traffic islands at xeriscape demonstration garden (*top left*), on a street with London Plane and Green Wave Yews (*top right*), and at intersection with Little Leaf Wintercreeper and Shademaster Honeylocust (*bottom*).

wholesale, the difference between wholesale and retail pays for the planting.) Always seek emergency funds from the finance committee for any unforeseen or emergency cost.

Public Opinion Surveys.   These should be conducted objectively to determine the public's perception of the department's shortcomings. A 0.1 percent or 2000-call survey is more than sufficient to determine the attitudes of the public and the major problems or strengths in the department.

Competitions.   If you are lucky enough to win one, the public will often refer to your award-winning department. The press coverage is always very positive.

Logos.   Most companies are known by their logo, such as IBM or GE. Municipal departments can capitalize on this as well. This presents an image the public will recognize as an organization that is on the top.

Champion Tree Program.   The public can be asked to assist in searching for the largest tree of a particular species in your community.

Publishing.   Any ideas, articles, awards, etc., should be published in any professional journal. This enhances the reputation of the department nationwide. Universities tell their professors to "publish or perish." The same should apply to municipal leaders.

Logo from Lexington, Massachusetts, Division of Parks and Trees.

Speakers. A series of prepared speakers should be available on popular arboricultural subjects. The speaker should be a municipal employee, well versed in the subject and having good speaking skills. The speaker should be available to address any local club, civic organization, group, meeting, or get-together where residents desire this information. The speaker should also be available to give talks at regional or national trade conferences where the municipality's reputation could be greatly enhanced.

Citizen-Activists. These people are valuable allies and promote urban forestry among other residents. They are especially useful for promoting and participating in tree planting, but they can also be asked to push support for the urban forestry budget at city hall and to conduct special programs that need volunteers.

Arbor Day Ceremonies

Arbor Day is the day to celebrate trees. National Arbor Day was founded in 1872 in Nebraska City by J. Sterling Morton. The idea grew from a statewide celebration in its first year to become a national holiday (although the date varies from state to state).

Municipal arborists must support their Arbor Day celebrations as well as other tree-related activities in their communities. It is an opportunity to accept gift trees and donated funds to purchase trees in memory or honor of someone or to mark a special event in their lives.

The typical annual program is held at a school, park, or city hall. The program should include opening remarks by the mayor, presentation of the Tree City—USA award by the state forester, and tree dedications by local groups and organizations. In some ceremonies, school students will sing several songs along with the school band, and some classes present plays about trees. Often programs present slide shows which emphasize the importance of the urban forests in terms of aesthetics, landscape value, wildlife habitat, energy conservation, pollution control, and how trees help balance the greenhouse effect and global warming. It should also emphasize good species and planting site selection as well as proper planting and maintenance procedures. Following the conclusion of the program, the students plant trees. In addition, children should be given a seedling to be planted at the site of their own choosing. Planting instructions are provided with each seedling, and students should be encouraged to maintain and care for the tree.

Local TV personalities can preside over the event, which might include a children's parade, salute to the flag, dedication of a peace tree and memorial plaque, speeches by several local officials, several songs and cultural dances. There could also be an Environmental Exposition with booths and displays, solar cars, health foods, student exhibits, organic gardening displays, outdoor walks, environmental photographs display, energy conservation displays, and a free-earth give-away of composted municipal leaf mold. The local newspapers can provide editorial support, articles, and an Arbor Day special supplement. The local television stations can cover special events and have environmental shows and public service announcements during Arbor Week.

Consider book displays about trees at community libraries, horticulture centers, etc. Radio talk shows and local television interview shows offer an opportunity for urban tree professionals and amateur enthusiasts alike to highlight the story of community forestry potential and problems.

Arbor Day is celebrated in many different ways in communities around the United States. Below are some specific programs that feature many of the ideas just mentioned.

Modesto, California.   The city of Modesto is very proud of the community involvement and support of the Arbor Day celebration as well as other tree-related activities. Citizens often donate funds to purchase trees in memory or honor of someone or to mark a special event in their lives. Modesto is also proud to be the recipient of the Tree City—USA award for several years. Special funding is used for the purchase, growing, and planting of trees for Arbor Day celebrations which include the planting of approximately 5000 trees annually.

A typical program is held at a local school. The program includes opening remarks by the mayor, presentation of a resolution from the State of California Assembly, presentation of the Tree City—USA award by the state forester's office, and tree dedications by local groups and organizations. Students sing several songs, accompanied by the school band, and one of the classes presents a play about the nearby "Calayeras Big Trees." Following the conclusion of the program, students plant trees throughout the schoolyard and park. In addition, each child is given a seedling to be planted at the site of his or her own choosing.

Not only are the forty-one employees of the Modesto Tree Division actively involved, but also local groups and organizations, students and parents, government officials, and private citizens participate in the program and in the planting of trees.

Fort Collins, Colorado.   Arbor Day is celebrated during the third week of April here. During this week, members of the city forestry division, Colorado State Forest Service, and the landscape industry visit fifth-grade classes in the local schools to present a slide show and distribute seedlings. The slide show emphasizes the importance of urban forests, good species and planting site selection, and proper planting and maintenance procedures.

An Arbor Day celebration is planned at an elementary school where community officials, students, and citizens gather to participate in a short ceremony to honor trees and to present the Tree City—USA award.

New Orleans, Louisiana.   Each year on or around Arbor Day, the New Orleans Parkway and Park Commission and its Parkway Partners Program offer to the Orleans parish schools a tree for Arbor Day. Founded in 1983, the Parkway Partners Program of New Orleans is a joint venture of citizens and government, working for the maintenance and beautification of the city's grounds, parks, and playgrounds.

Planting instructions are provided with each seedling, and students are encouraged to maintain and care for the tree. A tree sale is held each March by the Parkway and Parks Commission to encourage citizens to plant trees on public property.

Lakewood, Ohio.   The city of Lakewood celebrates Arbor Day by planting the Arbor Day Tree at a public park. The mayor, public officials, and children from local schools participate in the Arbor Day program by reading original poetry and stories about trees.

In addition, a tree identification program highlights the locations of the oldest trees in Lakewood, and they are identified with a plaque. Lakewood has a tree that is over 150 years old and has local historical significance.

The city of Lakewood has also been awarded Tree City—USA, for which it is extremely proud.

Parsippany, New Jersey.   Parsippany's Arbor Day ceremony is held at the municipal building. Parsippany has received the Tree City—USA award for many years. The presentation is made to the mayor by the state forester. During the ceremony, two trees are planted near the municipal building.

Each year, the Parsippany Parks and Forestry Department distributes approximately 1500 seedlings to all third-grade students. The department is assisted in the packaging of these seedlings by the local boy scout troops. Also teachers hold Arbor Day programs at many of the local schools.

Arbor Day activities and celebrations. *Middle:* In ribbon-cutting ceremony, two trees are used which are later planted in the sidewalk nearby.

San Jose, California. San Jose celebrates Arbor Day with a large ceremony at a local park. Local TV personalities preside over the event which includes a children's parade, salute to the flag, dedication of a peace tree and memorial plaque, speeches by several local officials, presentation of the Tree City—USA award, several songs and cultural dances, and the making of a multicultural patch quilt. There is also an Arbor Day registration table and other tables on which many different ethnic organizations have displays. The entire ceremony is sponsored by individual or organization contributors and organized by a sixteen-member committee.

Wellesley, Massachusetts. On Arbor Day, there is a Tree City— USA ceremony and tree plantings at every public and parochial school, a downtown tree planting project, and special tree planting ceremonies at several other locations. There have been as many as four Arbor Day or tree dedication ceremonies per year.

Winnipeg, Manitoba. Celebration of Arbor Day is carried out in conjunction with National Forest Week, which is held in Canada during the second week of May. National Forest Week includes a program which consists of setting up information booths at a local park with information available on horticultural problems, and seedlings are distributed to the public. Members of the Manitoba Legislature as well as all city councilors and the mayor receive a seedling.

Cedar Rapids, Iowa. For the past several years, Cedar Rapids has had fun with Arbor Day activities, moving to different parks and schools. Principals, teachers, and students are all glad to get outside for Arbor Day and tree planting activities, especially when travel is not necessary.

Mascots such as Woodsy Owl, Ricky Raccoon, and Smokey the Bear are a standard part of Arbor Day activities, which make popular media coverage. Youngsters of all ages are attracted to the animals representing environmental causes.

The mayor and other city officials participate in Arbor Day and Tree City—USA activities which involve national and state recognition. Political leaders enjoy attending noncontroversial events such as Arbor Day ceremonies.

During the month of April prior to Arbor Day, several displays are set up which speak to the many and various aspects of tree benefits and care: tree book displays at the community libraries; a tree poetry display at the community theater; a tree music display at the community orchestra theater; a flowering-tree display at the community horticulture center; and several others which tie trees to the specific interests of those using that facility. Even general tree displays in vacant storefronts and empty windows attracted the public's notice to the importance of trees.

Radio talk shows and local television interview shows offer an opportunity for urban tree professionals and amateur enthusiasts alike to highlight the story of community forestry potential and problems. Arbor Day serves as the cause-celebration for scheduling these activities so that important points are made at the beginning of the growing season, when most people have the greatest interest in the plant world and preventive activity can be carried out to reduce potential problems during stressful development periods.

Toledo, Ohio.   Toledo City Parks sponsors an Arbor Day poetry contest for local fourth graders and an Arbor Day logo contest for senior citizens who have a flair for the arts. The winning fourth graders received a tree planted in their honor on school property and have their poems published in the local paper.

At Toledo's Arbor Day awards ceremony, children and senior citizens are greeted by Smokey the Bear, the Toledo Hospital's Healthy Bear, and Lucas, mascot for Keep Toledo/Lucas County Beautiful. Following the awards ceremony, Arbor Day participants are invited to enjoy a series of hands-on workshops and operations displays by the Toledo Forestry Division. Sessions include interpreting a tree's age; milling operations; tree chipping and uses for the mulch; chain saw sculpturing; stump removal; a large tree trimming/removal operation; and proper planting techniques. Arbor Day concludes with the distribution of free seedlings to all participants for planting and nurturing at home.

In these times when people are concerned about global warming, the greenhouse effect, and green spaces in our urban areas, a day set aside to plant trees and to honor their contribution to the earth can be of great value in the effort to improve our living environment.

Tree City—USA

The Tree City—USA program is sponsored by the National Arbor Day Foundation and administered through the office of every state forester. The program began in 1976 and has had solid success and growth every year since. In 1985, 672 U.S. cities participated in the program. By 1991, the number of cities had jumped to 1300.

Tree City—USA communities take special interest in trees and the benefits trees provide. Trees are planted and maintained in parks and along streets for their beauty and shade; to attract wildlife; to reduce noise, wind, and glare; and to increase property values. Many Tree City—USA communities have initiated extensive replanting programs to replace dead or diseased trees. Some communities focus on special tree planting programs for beautifying specific areas of the community. Most Tree City—USA communities prune and maintain all public trees as a part of their management program.

The most important part of the Tree City—USA program, however, is the opportunity to build strong positive working relationships between residents and local governments and their public trees. People like trees. Tree City—USA is an urban tree program that provides recognition that local government is working to support the interests of residents and their tree care program.

The Tree City—USA award is given to communities that meet four requirements: (1) The community must have a legally authorized tree board or department; (2) it must have a community tree ordinance or by-law; (3) it must have a comprehensive forestry program supported by a minimum of $2 per capita; (4) it must make an Arbor Day proclamation and a public ceremony or commemorative tree planting. The application deadline is December 31 of each year.

The benefits of the program are many. The entire community can become aware of the program because of its popular, catchy title. Residents are reminded of the program because of the Tree City—USA flag that flies in the community center and signs posted at the community's entrances. The awards program and Arbor Day ceremonies are a favorite with politicians because everyone likes trees, appreciates their value, and is willing to support planting and proper maintenance of valuable public trees.

Champion Trees

Champion trees are also known as *great trees* or *big trees,* and records on these trees are kept by American Forests (AF). There is something about a big tree that commands respect. Trees are the largest and oldest living organisms, with the oldest being a Bristlecone Pine in the Sierra Nevadas of southern California. It is 4600 years old.

There is a lot of public interest in champion trees. Some communities have capitalized on this interest, and they have started a search. They first look over the public trees indicated on the street tree inventory. They then go public and invite everyone to look for large trees throughout the municipality. Public announcements are made in the local press for about 3 months as calls are accepted and trees are measured. This effort results in the nomination of trees that can become state champions.

The public appreciation of this effort is widespread, and it encourages a lot of interest from adults as well as children. Phone calls with nominations continue coming in for months after the search ends. Teachers in the public schools and instructors at local colleges find this program to be an excellent learning tool for plant identification as well as mathematics.

AF's program is over 50 years old. The National Register of Big Trees has grown from 100 big trees in 1940 to 850 native and naturalized species today. Only five trees on the original list are still champions today.

To nominate a tree, you must correctly identify the species or variety, measure the circumference in inches at 4.5 feet, calculate or measure the height to the nearest foot, and finally determine the average crown spread. Nominations are judged on a point system established by AF. One point is awarded for each inch of circumference, one point per foot of height, and one-fourth point per foot of crown spread. The three measurements are added to give a total point score. Circumference is the most important factor, followed by height and crown spread. If two trees of the same species have identical total point scores, the one with the larger circumference is named champion. All this information plus data about the location, owner, measurements taken, date, photographs, state of preservation, and nominator's name should be sent to the state forester or AF's National Register of Big Trees, P.O. Box 2000, Washington, DC 20013.

Think about announcing a search in your city to get your residents involved.

Sources

Brudney, Jeffrey L.: *Fostering Volunteer Programs in the Public Sector*, Jossey-Bass Publishers, San Francisco, 1990.

Fazio, James R.: "Tree City—USA Growth Awards," *Arbor Day*, May/June 1991, p. 4.

Fazio, James R.: "Ten Years of Tree City—USA," *Arbor Day*, May/June 1986, p. 4.

Forgacs, Sandra: "Public Relations Programs," *City Trees*, November 1986, p. 9.

"Great Trees of Wichita—Sedgwick County," Sedgwick County Extension Service, Wichita, n.d.

Mah-Kooyman, Shirley: "Volunteers, Establishment and

A 72-inch-diameter, 180-foot-tall Blue Gum Eucalyptus globulus. (*Photo courtesy Robert Allen Photography.*)

Facilitation of a Valuable Resource," *City Trees*, January/February 1991, p. 18.

"National Register of Big Trees—America's Living Landmarks," *American Forests*, January/February 1990, p. 2.

Phillips, L. E., Jr.: "Champion Tree Program," *City Trees*, March/April 1991, p. 7.

Phillips, Leonard E., Jr.: "Arbor Day Programs for 1990," *City Trees*, March/April 1990, May/June 1990, p. 5.

Phillips, Leonard E., Jr.: "Public Relations Programs Continued," *City Trees*, November 1986, p. 10.

Phillips, Leonard E., Jr.: "Protecting Street Trees," *City Trees*, May 1983, p. 10.

8

The Abridged Plan

Some communities may feel that their entire master planning process is too expensive, will be too overwhelming to undertake, or will take too long. They may also feel the document will not be used, will be a waste of money, contains information that may never be used, and will need constant updating, all with questionable value. To help these communities, an *abridged plan* can be prepared, provided everyone involved fully acknowledges that it is less comprehensive and therefore should be used only as a general guide and not as a policy or maintenance document.

The abridged plan will contain many of the same elements as the comprehensive street tree master plan. For example, there will be an inventory, but it will be the rapid sample survey, much like a Gallup poll for street trees. The abridged plan will also need a street tree planting plan, it must follow the diversification formula, and it should eventually lead to the establishment of street tree regulations and a tree advisory committee.

Inventory

Rapid Street Tree Inventory

The rapid sample survey consists of a random collection of information for about 2000 trees which is then statistically calculated, with 95 percent accuracy, to become the inventory of any size city. The information collected is basically the same as that for a complete inventory. Typical items of information to be collected include species; dbh classes in 6- or 12-inch increments; condition in three or four classes; and other aspects that may be important to the local community such as location, maintenance needs, and vacancies. The rapid sample survey is conducted in an unbiased, random manner.

To begin the inventory, the city is divided into two levels. The first level defines regions within the city such as business districts, residential areas, etc., while the second level examines 20 to 50 city blocks within each region. Areas of forests and areas containing no trees are excluded. Each region is treated separately.

A presample is done first, to determine the average size of a block within each region. At the same time, the number of trees per block is counted. Once an average number of trees per block is known, the number of trees can be calculated. Once the average perimeter per block is calculated, this information can be used to measure the length of curvilinear streets within the city. However, since only the interior block is surveyed in the city block section, both sides of the street are counted in the curvilinear sections. Half the perimeter length is equal to a curvilinear section.

After the presample is completed, all the blocks and curvilinear streets are identified and assigned a number on a map. A random selection process identifies which blocks or streets will be surveyed in more depth. The survey information is gathered by four people driving around the block . The driver has the street maps, while two people observe features of each tree, such as species and condition by one observer and size, location, number, and other data by the other observer. The fourth person records the information into a tape recorder or hand-held computer. This process continues until 2000 trees are counted. This inventory process can be done in 2 or 3 days.

All the information is entered in an inventory program in a computer, and a complete inventory is calculated. Illustrations on pages 182 and 183 clarify the rapid sample street tree survey.

Other Components

Abridged Plan Tree List

The tree list should be prepared, as it is in the comprehensive plan, to indicate which trees should be planted in the community. The trees on this list should be carefully chosen, and this selection is based on the tree's tolerance to the local environment and hardiness. Many of the varieties can be new selections that are recommended for street tree locations. They are often better than the species in terms of pest tolerance, shape, foliage, flower, storm damage resistance, etc. Remove from the list any trees known from experience to be susceptible to storm damage or to have high maintenance costs, poor fruiting habits, shallow root development, and other problems associated with urban trees.

The diversification formula should be followed so that for every 100 trees planted, no more than 10 trees of any one family and no more than 5 trees of any one species should be planted.

As in the regular street tree master planning process, the diversification formula should be carried one step further. It should be applied to the existing street tree inventory so that the dependence on a single species from previous plantings or natural plantings will not be carried forward into future plantings. Assuming there are 50,000 existing trees in the street tree inventory, all families of trees containing 5000 trees should be avoided on the planting list as well as all species of trees containing more than 2500 trees. Furthermore, by keeping the inventory up to date through either a comprehensive inventory or the rapid sample survey, the total tree count can be frequently checked against the diversification formula to prevent a creeping dependency on a single species.

Protecting Street Trees with Regulations

Even the abridged plan requires that every municipality establish policies related to the care of street trees. These policies should be approved by the community's tree policy-making board or elected officials. Consideration should also be given to a review of policies relating to trees by municipal boards such as the planning board. Many states have laws enabling municipalities to improve protection for street trees, and many states protect public trees directly through state law. Additional information specific to the laws and regulations of the individual community will vary considerably from community to community, so every forester or tree superintendent and the tree advisory committee members should know the laws and regulations available for their use and be able to expand these laws in the interest of the community's shade tree environment.

Conclusion

Many have recently been overwhelmed by cries in the press about the greenhouse effect, global warming, and the declining ozone layer. Since there is little that most of us can do about this problem in the Amazon rain forest, we should concentrate on solving this problem locally, where we live, by planting and properly maintaining as many trees as possible.

This municipal street tree master plan should be developed to justify an expanded tree planting program, to enhance the beauty of

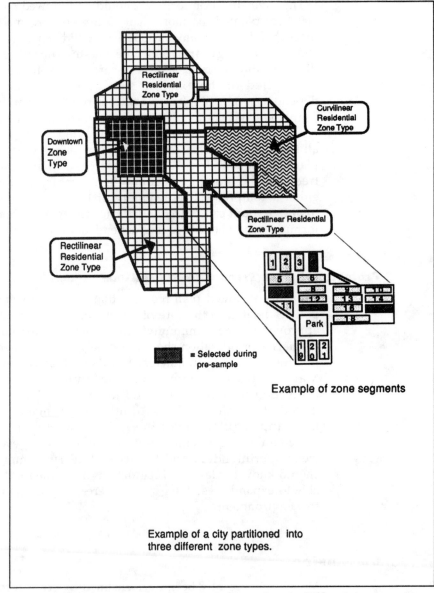

Rectilinear Residential Zone Type

Curvilinear Residential Zone Type

Downtown Zone Type

Rectilinear Residential Zone Type

Rectilinear Residential Zone Type

≡ Selected during pre-sample

Example of zone segments

Example of a city partitioned into three different zone types.

Example of a city partitioned into three different zone types.

Typical Block

Blocks A & B average
1750 linear feet each.

Trees on these blocks are
observed on inside of the
perimeter only.

Curvilinear Street

Block C measures
875 linear feet.

Trees on this block are
observed on both sides
of the street.

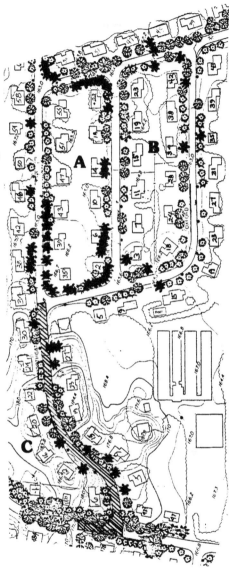

the community and the health and welfare of its citizens, to care for the existing municipal tree canopy, and to replace the declining population of street trees.

Source

Bassuk, Nina, and Richard Jaenson: "Rapid New Method to Inventory Street Trees," *City Trees*, January/February 1992, p. 10.

Detailed Description of Recommended Trees

DESCRIPTION

Common name: | **Queen Elizabeth Maple**

Botanical name: | *Acer campestre* 'Queen Elizabeth'

Parentage: | Cultivar of Hedge Maple

Hardiness zone: | 4

Mature size: | Height: 35 feet
Spread: 30 feet

Plant patent: | 4392

UNIQUE FEATURES

Flower: | Greenish

Fruit: | Dense, 1- to 1.5-inch samaras

Foliage: | Golden yellow autumn color, dark green glossy foliage

Left: Juvenile. *Middle:* Adult. *Right:* Shrub form.

Bark:	Corky stems, pubescent twigs
Growth rate:	Dense growth, slow rate
Site requirements:	Dry conditions, sandy to clay loam soil
Pest and disease resistance:	Relatively free of pests
Tolerance:	Tolerant of air pollution and drought
Other comments:	Excellent screen planting or hedge, excellent for under wires, transplants easily

AVAILABLE FROM

Lake County Nursery, Inc., Perry, OH, and several other nurseries

DESCRIPTION

Common name:	**Celebration Maple**
Botanical name:	*Acer freemani* 'Celebration'

Parentage (if hybrid):	*A. rubrum* x *A. saccharinum*
Hardiness zone:	4
Mature size:	Height: 45 feet Spread: 20 to 25 feet Shape: compact, upright
Plant patent:	Applied for

UNIQUE FEATURES

Flower:	Red
Fruit:	Seedless
Foliage:	Green, dense, red to gold in autumn
Growth rate:	Uniform growth, fast when young
Site requirements:	Tolerant of wet soil, heat, and drought; sandy to clay soil; sun to shade

Acer x 'Celebration'. (*Photo courtesy Lake County Nursery.*)

Pest and disease resistance:	Excellent
Storm resistance:	Strong crotch angles

AVAILABLE FROM

Lake County Nursery, Perry, OH
Bailey Nurseries, Inc., St. Paul, MN
Carlton Plants, Dayton, OR
Femrite Nursery Co., Aurora, OR
Schichtel's, Orchard Park, NY
Speer & Sons Nursery, Inc., Hillsboro, OR

DESCRIPTION

Common name:	**Paperbark Maple**
Botanical name:	*Acer griseum*
Parentage:	Introduced in 1900s from China
Hardiness zone:	5
Mature size:	Height: 25 feet Spread: 20 feet

UNIQUE FEATURES

Flower:	Few flowers
Fruit:	Sterile seed
Foliage:	Soft green, silver underside, bright red-orange in autumn
Bark:	Cinnamon-colored underbark exposed by exfoliating outer bark

Acer griseum. (Photo courtesy Wayside Gardens.)

Growth rate:	Compact
Site requirements:	Rich, silty loam; well-drained, sunny
Pest and disease resistance:	Very few problems

AVAILABLE FROM

Many nurseries

DESCRIPTION

Common name:	**Cleveland Norway Maple**
Botanical name:	*Acer platanoides* 'Cleveland'
Parentage:	Cultivar of Norway Maple
Hardiness zone:	3
Mature size:	Height: 50 to 60 feet Spread: 25 feet

UNIQUE FEATURES

Flower:	Greenish-yellow, early in spring
Fruit:	Abundant samaras
Foliage:	Large, dense dark green, golden yellow in autumn
Root growth:	Shallow, can heave sidewalks
Bark:	Olive, brown
Growth rate:	Vigorous, upright habit
Site requirements:	Silty to clay loam, sun, tolerates summer heat
Pest and disease resistance:	Very few problems
Salt tolerance:	Excellent
Other comments:	Tolerates heat and wide range of soils, easy to transplant, oval, upright habit

AVAILABLE FROM

Some nurseries

DESCRIPTION

Common name:	**Summershade Norway Maple**
Botanical name:	*Acer platanoides* 'Summershade'
Parentage:	Selection made in 1958
Hardiness zone:	3

Mature size:	Height: 60 feet Spread: 40 feet
Plant patent:	1748

UNIQUE FEATURES

Flower:	Small yellow clusters, before leaves
Fruit:	2-inch winged samara
Foliage:	Large, dense leaves, bright green in summer, golden yellow in autumn, leathery
Bark:	Olive, brown, smooth
Growth rate:	Rapid
Root structure and depth:	Very shallow-rooted; plant away from sidewalks
Site requirements:	Excellent heat resistance, drought-tolerant
Pest and disease resistance:	Excellent
Storm resistance:	Windburn resistance
Salt resistance:	Excellent
Other comments:	Upright habit, single leader

AVAILABLE FROM

Lake County Nursery, Perry, OH
Princeton Nursery, Princeton, NJ

DESCRIPTION

Common name:	**Red Sunset Red Maple**

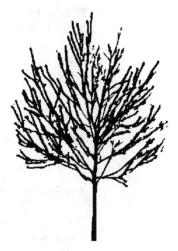

Botanical name: *Acer rubrum* 'Red Sunset'

Hardiness zone: 3

Mature size: Height: 45 to 50 feet
                                   Spread: 35 to 40 feet

UNIQUE FEATURES

Flower: Red, profuse

Fruit: Winged samaras, bright red

Foliage: Brilliant orange, red in
                                   autumn, dark green and
                                   glossy in summer

Bark: Silvery color for winter
                                   interest

Growth rate: Vigorous

Root structure: Transplants easily

Site requirements:	Moist conditions, tolerates most soils and urban pollution
Pest and disease resistance:	Excellent
Storm resistance:	Somewhat weak-wooded in ice storms
Other comments:	Oval, upright crown, one of the best Red Maples

AVAILABLE FROM

Most nurseries

DESCRIPTION

Common name:	**Karpick Maple**
Botanical name:	*Acer rubrum* 'Karpick'
Parentage:	Selection from Red Maple
Hardiness zone:	4
Mature size:	Height: 45 feet Spread: 20 feet

UNIQUE FEATURES

Flower:	Red, small and profuse, typical of species
Fruit:	Bright red samaras
Foliage:	Brilliant reds to yellow in

	autumn, rich green color
Bark:	Distinctive red twigs
Growth rate:	Rapid, uniform, upright
Site requirements:	Moist, silty loam soil
Pest and disease resistance:	Typical of species
Storm resistance:	Moderate, excellent municipal tree
Other comments:	Named for Frank E. Karpick, former city forester of Buffalo, New York, and first SMA president

AVAILABLE FROM

Schichtel's Nursery, Orchard Park, NY

DESCRIPTION

Common name:	**Endowment Columnar Sugar Maple**
Botanical name:	*Acer saccharum* 'Endowment Columnar'
Parentage (if hybrid):	Seedling selection
Hardiness zone:	4
Mature size:	Height: 35 to 40 feet Spread: 12 to 16 feet
Plant patent:	4654

UNIQUE FEATURES

Flower:	Not of ornamental importance
Fruit:	Not of ornamental importance
Foliage:	Orange red fall color, no summer scorch
Bark:	No frost crack
Growth rate:	Rapid
Root structure and depth:	Good; good transplantability
Pest and disease resistance:	No disease or pest problems
Storm resistance:	Excellent
Salt tolerance:	Unknown
Other comments:	Good results from planting under high summer heat and light stress

AVAILABLE FROM

The Siebenthaler Company, Dayton, OH
Manbeck Nurseries, Inc., New Knoxville, OH
Speer & Sons Nursery, Inc., Hillsboro, OR

DESCRIPTION

Common name:	**Green Mountain Sugar Maple**
Botanical name:	*Acer saccharum* 'Green Mountain'

Parentage:	Selection of Sugar Maple, found in 1964
Hardiness zone:	3
Mature size:	Height: 50 to 75 feet Spread: 40 to 60 feet
Plant patent:	2339

UNIQUE FEATURES

Flower:	Average with leaves, greenish yellow
Fruit:	Typical samaras
Foliage:	Dark green, turns orange and scarlet in autumn, twice the thickness to resist urban stress, and seldom gets leaf scorch
Bark:	Gray and furrowed
Growth rate:	Slowest of the maples
Site requirements:	Will tolerate dry, windy summer and compact soils
Pest and disease resistance:	Most tolerant of Sugar Maples, scorch-resistant
Storm resistance:	Best of all maples
Other comments:	Oval crown, considered by many to be the best maple for street tree use

AVAILABLE FROM

Princeton Nursery, Princeton, NJ

Acer saccharum 'Green Mountain'. (*Photo courtesy G. M. Biel for Princeton Nursery.*)

Several other nurseries

DESCRIPTION

Common name:	**Tatarian Maple**
Botanical name:	*Acer tataricum*
Parentage:	Introduced in 1759
Hardiness zone:	4
Mature size:	Height: 20 to 30 feet Spread: 20 feet

UNIQUE FEATURES

Flower:	Greenish, white

Fruit:	Red samaras
Foliage:	Fine, light green, red to yellow in autumn
Bark:	Brown
Growth rate:	Moderate
Root structure and depth:	Transplant balled and burlapped
Site requirements:	Very adaptable and tolerates most sites
Pest and disease resistance:	Excellent
Other comments:	Upright, elliptical habit

AVAILABLE FROM

Lake County Nursery, Perry, OH
Princeton Nursery, Princeton, NJ

DESCRIPTION

Common name:	**Heritage Birch**
Botanical name:	*Betula nigra* 'Heritage'
Parentage (if hybrid):	Cultivar
Hardiness zone:	5
Mature size:	Height: 45 to 50 feet Spread: 30 to 40 feet
Plant patent:	4409

UNIQUE FEATURES

Flower:	Insignificant

Betula nigra 'Heritage'. (*Photo courtesy Bobtown Nursery.*)

Fruit:	Typical of River Birch
Foliage:	Leathery texture, glossy dark green upper, light green under, yellow in autumn
Bark:	Tan to white when young, creamy to parchment white when mature, exfoliating bark
Growth rate:	Vigorous and robust
Root structure and depth:	Typical of River Birch
Pest and disease resistance:	Resistant to bronze birch borer
Storm resistance:	Resistant to wind and ice damage due to stout branching habit; does not weep like River Birch
Salt tolerance:	Fair, typical River Birch
Other comments:	Useful in parks, residential areas, and city streets; good for clumps or single specimen

AVAILABLE FROM

Bobtown Nursery, Onanock, VA
Princeton Nursery, Princeton, NJ

DESCRIPTION

Common name:	**Pyramidal European Hornbeam**
Botanical name:	*Carpinus betulus fastigiata*
Parentage:	Introduced from Europe in colonial times

Hardiness zone:	4
Mature size:	Height: 35 to 50 feet Spread: 15 feet

UNIQUE FEATURES

Flower:	Catkins
Fruit:	Small nutlets
Foliage:	Large dark green leaves, yellow in autumn, persistent over winter
Bark:	Gray, smooth
Growth rate:	Moderate, difficult to move when large, transplant balled and burlapped in spring
Site requirements:	Medium loam, moist, sun or part shade, pH of 6.0 to 7.5
Pest and disease resistance:	Excellent, except for two-line chestnut borer in block plantings
Salt tolerance:	Poor
Other comments:	Pyramidal in youth, rounded at maturity, withstands shearing, dense branching

AVAILABLE FROM

Most nurseries

DESCRIPTION

Common name:	**Magnifica Hackberry**

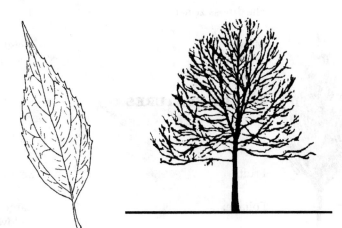

Botanical name:	*Celtis occidentalis* 'Magnifica'
Parentage (if hybrid):	*Laevigata* x *occidentalis*
Hardiness zone:	6
Mature size:	Height: 60 to 80 feet Spread: 60 to 80 feet
Plant patent:	2795

UNIQUE FEATURES

Fruit:	Orange-red to blue-black, sweet and loved by birds
Foliage:	Dark green, 2 to 4 inches long
Bark:	Smooth and gray
Growth rate:	Medium to fast
Root structure and depth:	Dense and fibrous, withstands compaction
Pest and disease resistance:	Resistant to witches'-broom and Dutch Elm disease
Drought resistance:	Excellent

Storm resistance:	Excellent
Salt tolerance:	Excellent
Other comments:	Rounded shape and pendulous branching; best grown in south and midwest

AVAILABLE FROM

Princeton Nursery, Princeton, NJ

DESCRIPTION

Common name:	**Prairie Pride Hackberry**
Botanical name:	*Celtis occidentalis* 'Prairie Pride'
Parentage:	Selection by Wandell's Nursery
Hardiness zone:	3
Mature size:	Height: 40 to 60 feet Spread: 35 feet
Plant patent:	3771

UNIQUE FEATURES

Flower:	Inconspicuous
Fruit:	Round drupe, orange-red, lighter than species
Foliage:	Similar to elms, dark green and glossy, thick and leathery, golden yellow in autumn
Bark:	Narrow corky ridges, gray

Growth rate:	Medium
Root structure and depth:	Easily transplanted
Site requirements:	Tolerates dry soil and wind, sun or shady site, pH of 6.0 to 7.5; tolerates urban sites and adverse conditions
Pest and disease resistance:	Resistant to witches'-broom, but there are other pests
Other comments:	Rounded shape, uniform, and compact

AVAILABLE FROM

Lake County Nursery, Percy, OH

DESCRIPTION

Common name:	**Katsura Tree**
Botanical name:	*Cercidiphyllum japonicum*
Parentage (if hybrid):	Introduced in 1865 from Japan
Hardiness zone:	4
Mature size:	Height: 60 feet Spread: 40 feet

UNIQUE FEATURES

Flower:	Inconspicuous, sexes on separate trees
Fruit:	Small dry capsules, persistent over winter

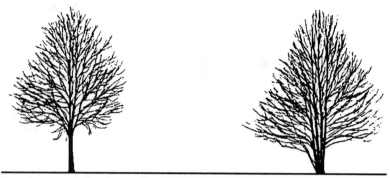

Tree form at left, clump form at right.

Foliage: Fine texture, heart-shaped leaves, yellow in autumn, 4-inch-long leaves, new leaves reddish

Growth rate: Fast when young, slower with age

Site requirements: Rich loam, moist soil, sun or partial shade

Pest and disease resistance: Excellent

Other comments: Very clean tree

AVAILABLE FROM

Most nurseries

DESCRIPTION

Common name: **Fringe tree**

Botanical name: *Chionanthus virginicus*

Parentage (if hybrid): Native

Hardiness zone: 4

Mature size:	Height: 30 feet Spread: 25 feet

UNIQUE FEATURES

Flower:	White, loose panicles, profuse threadlike petals, bloom in June, fragrant
Fruit:	Dark blue clusters, persistent
Foliage:	Appears very late in spring, bright yellow in autumn, large dark green leaves
Growth rate:	Slow
Site requirements:	Sunny, moist sandy loam, tolerates shade
Pest and disease resistance:	Scale insects are only problem
Other comments:	Deep-rooted, planted in groups to promote fruiting

AVAILABLE FROM

Most nurseries

DESCRIPTION

Common name:	**Yellowwood**
Botanical name:	*Cladrastis lutca*
Parentage (if hybrid):	Native
Hardiness zone:	3
Mature size:	Height: 50 feet Spread: 40 feet

UNIQUE FEATURES

Flower: White, pendulous clusters, early summer, fragrant

Fruit: Long, thin, beanlike pods which turn brown, persistent

Foliage: Dense, orange to yellow in autumn

Bark: Smooth, light gray, often multistemmed

Growth rate: Fairly fast

Site requirements: Needs space, rich soil, good drainage

Pest and disease resistance: Excellent

Storm resistance: Generally excellent although some reports indicate weak wood in major storms

Other comments: Bleeds heavily if pruned in spring

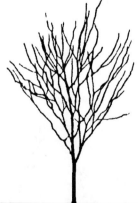

AVAILABLE FROM

Most nurseries

DESCRIPTION

Common name:	**President Ford Variegated Dogwood**
Botanical name:	*Cornus florida* 'President Gerald R. Ford'
Parentage:	*Cornus florida* seedling
Hardiness zone:	6
Mature size:	Typical of the species, 25 feet tall, wide, upright
Plant patent:	Registered

UNIQUE FEATURES

Flower:	White
Fruit:	Red
Foliage:	Large two-tone yellow outer border leaves, two-tone inner green turning to orange, keeping yellow and orange in fall even after two or three frosts
Bark:	Young growth tends to be yellowish green in first year, turning to regular color as it ages
Growth rate:	10 to 15 inches of top growth per year
Site requirements:	Sunny for best coloring, while

Cornus florida 'President Ford'.

shade will produce green foliage

Pest and disease resistance:

At present seems resistant to canker

Storm resistance:

Good

Other comments:

As plants age, there appear many areas of solid yellow leaves and yellow branches; and with appearance of solid yellowing, it may prove a little harder to transplant. In this case, a slight bit of shade may be in order.

AVAILABLE FROM

J. Verkade Nursery, Asbury, NJ

DESCRIPTION

Common name:

Summer Stars Dogwood

Botanical name:

Cornus kousa 'Summer Stars'

Parentage (if hybrid):

Selection of Japanese Dogwood

Hardiness zone:

5

Cornus kousa 'Summer Stars'. (*Photo courtesy Princeton Nursery.*)

Mature size:	Height: 20 feet Spread: 20 feet
Plant patent:	3090

UNIQUE FEATURES

Flower:	Inconspicuous in center of large pointed bracts, creamy white, July and August
Fruit:	Strawberrylike, red, attracts birds
Foliage:	Dense, scarlet in autumn color
Bark:	Attractive, mottled
Growth rate:	Rapid
Site requirements:	Sun or partial shade, moist, high-organic soil
Pest and disease resistance:	Resistant to disease and insects
Other comments:	Distinctive horizontal branches

AVAILABLE FROM

Princeton Nursery, Princeton, NJ
Wayside Gardens, Hodges, SC

DESCRIPTION

Common name: **Turkish Hazelnut**

Botanical name: *Corylus colurna*

Parentage (if hybrid):   Introduced in 1852

Hardiness zone: 4

Mature size: Height: 50 feet
                                      Spread: 25 feet

UNIQUE FEATURES

Flower: Catkins in winters

Fruit: Small nut

Foliage: Dark green, yellow to purple
                                      in autumn

Bark: Brown, scales, orange-brown
                                      under scales

Growth rate: Medium

Site requirements: Thrives in hot summers and
                                      cold winters, well-drained
                                      loam, scorch-resistant,
                                      tolerates city conditions

Pest and disease resistance: Excellent

Root structure and depth: Difficult to transplant

AVAILABLE FROM

Princeton Nursery, Princeton, NJ

DESCRIPTION

Common name:	**Washington Hawthorn**
Botanical name:	*Crataegus phaenopyrum*
Parentage (if hybrid):	Native
Hardiness zone:	4
Mature size:	Height: 30 feet Spread: 10 to 15 feet

Crataegus phaenopyrum. (Photo courtesy Princeton Nursery.)

UNIQUE FEATURES

Flower:	White $\frac{1}{4}$-inch diameter in clusters, mid-June
Fruit:	Bright red, $\frac{1}{4}$-inch diameter, persistent all winter
Foliage:	Dense, glossy, deep green, scarlet to orange in autumn
Bark:	Dense, twiggy growth, sharp spines
Growth rate:	Moderate to fast
Site requirements:	Medium loam, moist, sun or part shade
Pest and disease resistance:	Moderate to good
Other comments:	Good for city sites, specify tree form to minimize thorn problem

Tree form at left, shrub form at right.

AVAILABLE FROM

Most nurseries

DESCRIPTION

Common name:	**Hardy Rubber tree**
Botanical name:	*Eucommia ulmoides*
Parentage:	Introduced from China in 1896
Hardiness zone:	4
Mature size:	Height: 40 to 60 feet Spread: 40 to 50 feet

UNIQUE FEATURES

Flower:	Inconspicuous, sexes separate
Fruit:	Few to none
Foliage:	Dark green, large, glossy
Bark:	Gray brown, elastic strings

run from injured or cut bark,
bark ridged and furrowed in
old age

Growth rate:

Medium

Root structure:

Transplants easily

Site requirements:

Tolerant of most soils and
drought; pH of 6.0 to 7.5

Pest and disease resistance:

Excellent

Salt tolerance:

Tolerant of urban conditions

Other comments:

Rounded shape, not
especially ornamental

AVAILABLE FROM

Many nurseries

DESCRIPTION

Common name:

Franklin Tree

Botanical name:

Franklinia altamaha

Parentage:

Native

Hardiness zone:

6

Mature size:

Height: 20 feet; best if grown
as shrub to combat winter cold
Spread: 15 feet

UNIQUE FEATURES

Flower:

White 2- to 3-inch five-petaled
gold center, blooms in
summer and fall

The Franklin tree, *Franklinia altamaha,* sometimes known as the "lost camellia," is classified as one of the rarest trees in the world, which may explain why relatively few people know of this native ornamental. Once found only in the wilds of southeastern Georgia in a very small area along the banks of the Altamaha River, the historic *Franklinia* was discovered there by botanist John Bartram in 1765 and named for his friend Benjamin Franklin. It is no longer found in its natural setting and was last seen around 1800. All plants today are said to be from Bartram's 1765 collection. (*Photo courtesy Princeton Nursery.*)

Buds:	Small green buds, change to white when opening, $\frac{3}{4}$-inch diameter
Fruit:	$\frac{1}{2}$ inch, nutlike
Foliage:	4 to 6 inches, medium to dark green, pink, red to orange in autumn
Bark:	Striped when young, fissured with age
Growth rate:	18 to 24 inches per year
Site requirements:	Sun, tolerant of most acidic soils
Pest and disease resistance:	Excellent with little or no pest problems, root rot when in wet soil
Salt tolerance:	Unknown
Other comments:	Medium-density appearance

AVAILABLE FROM

DeWitt Farms Nursery, Bryson City, NC
Princeton Nursery, Princeton, NJ
Some other nurseries

DESCRIPTION

Common name:	**Hesse European Ash**
Botanical name:	*Fraxinus excelsior* 'Hessei'
Hardiness zone:	3
Mature size:	Height: 60 feet Spread: 40 feet

UNIQUE FEATURES

Flower: Insignificant

Fruit: Seedless

Foliage: Single, not compound typical
                                of ash, dark green, leathery,
                                yellow in autumn

Growth rate: Rapid, vigorous

Site requirements: Adapts to most soil
                                conditions

Pest and disease resistance: Moderate to good

Storm resistance: Excellent, durable wood

AVAILABLE FROM

Lake County Nursery, Perry, OH
Schichtel's Nursery, Orchard Park, NY

DESCRIPTION

Common name: **Summit Ash**

Botanical name: *Fraxinus pennsylvania*
                                'Summit'

Parentage (if hybrid):   Variety of *F. pennsylvania*

Hardiness zone: 3

Mature size: Height: 60 feet
                                Spread: 30 feet

UNIQUE FEATURES

Flower: Staminate

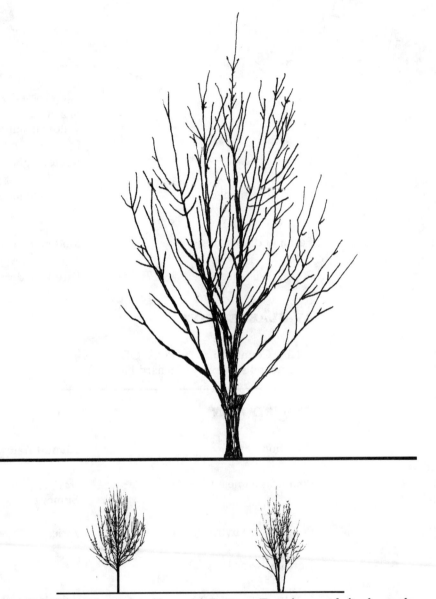

Fraxinus pennsylvania lanceolata 'Summit'. Bottom: Tree form at left, clump form at right.

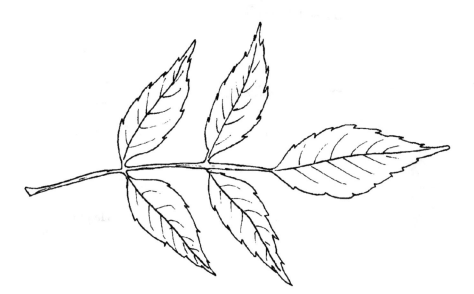

Fruit:	Seedless
Foliage:	Glossy, orange-yellow in autumn
Bark:	Uniform, straight trunk
Growth rate:	Strong central leader, relatively fast growth, oval crown
Site requirements:	Medium loam, moist, sun, tolerates most soils
Pest and disease resistance:	Susceptible to borers and other insects, ash decline, and leaf spots
Other comments:	Best of the seedless Green Ash, and superior replacement for Marshall's Ash

AVAILABLE FROM

Most nurseries

DESCRIPTION

Common name:	**Princeton Sentry Ginkgo**
Botanical name:	*Ginkgo biloba* 'Princeton Sentry'
Parentage (if hybrid):	Selection from *Ginkgo biloba*, grafted male
Hardiness zone:	4
Mature size:	Height: 75 feet Spread: 20 feet
Plant patent:	2726

UNIQUE FEATURES

Ginkgo biloba 'Princeton Sentry'. (*Photo courtesy Princeton Nursery.*)

Flower:	Male only
Fruit:	Male only
Foliage:	Bright green, brilliant yellow in autumn, large fan-shaped leaves
Bark:	Typical of species
Growth rate:	Rapid and long-lived
Root structure and depth:	Dense, fibrous roots, easily transplanted
Site requirements:	Rich sandy loam, moist, well-drained, sun
Pest and disease resistance:	Free from all pests
Salt tolerance:	Good
Other comments:	Columnar, tolerates dust and smoke

AVAILABLE FROM

Princeton Nursery, Princeton, NJ
Bailey Nurseries, Inc., St. Paul, MN
Some other nurseries

DESCRIPTION

Common name:	**Shademaster Honeylocust**
Botanical name:	*Gleditsia triacanthos inermis* 'Shademaster'
Parentage (if hybrid):	Cultivar developed in 1956
Hardiness zone:	4
Mature size:	Height: 40 feet Spread: 35 feet
Plant patent:	1515

UNIQUE FEATURES

Gleditsia triacanthos inermis 'Shademaster'. (*Photo courtesy Princeton Nursery.*)

Flower:	Small, greenish racemes
Fruit:	Very few long twisted pods
Foliage:	Fine texture, dark green, yellow in autumn
Bark:	Straight trunk, ascending branches
Growth rate:	Rapid
Root structure and depth:	Deep fibrous roots, easily transplanted
Site requirements:	Adapts to wide range of growing conditions, sun, moist, rich loam

Pest and disease resistance:	Moderate to disease, excellent to pests
Storm resistance:	Excellent
Other comments:	No thorns, casts light shade, drought-resistant

AVAILABLE FROM

Most nurseries

DESCRIPTION

Common name:	**Winter Red Winterberry**
Botanical name:	*Ilex verticillata* 'Winter Red'
Parentage (if hybrid):	Cultivar
Hardiness zone:	4
Mature size:	Height: 8 to 10 feet Spread: 6 to 8 feet
Plant patent:	29912

UNIQUE FEATURES

Flower:	Male and female required for fruiting
Fruit:	Heavy fruiting with large brilliant red berries; berries stay red after others turn black and persist until spring
Foliage:	Rich and dark green, long-lasting foliage turns bronze in fall

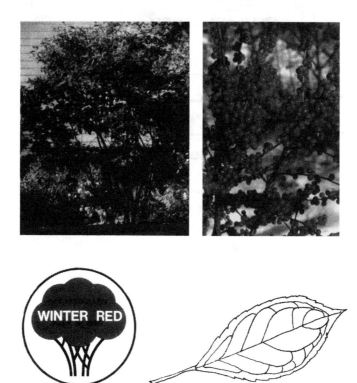

Ilex verticillata 'Winter Red'. (*Photo courtesy Bobtown Nursery.*)

Bark:	Forms new multiple stems as it matures
Growth rate:	Responds to nitrogen fertilizer with darker green foliage and heavier fruiting
Site requirements:	Grows well in moist areas and will tolerate shade
Pest and disease resistance:	Practically disease-free
Storm resistance:	Stout branching habit, resists damage
Other comments:	Useful in parks and city streets, requires minimum care

AVAILABLE FROM

Bobtown Nursery, Onanock, VA
Wayside Gardens, Hodges, SC
Weston Nurseries, Hopkinton, MA
Many other nurseries

DESCRIPTION

Common name:	**Moraine Sweetgum***
Botanical name:	*Liquidambar styraciflua* 'Moraine'
Parentage (if hybrid):	Seedling selection
Hardiness zone:	4
Mature size:	Height: 35 to 40 feet Spread: 25 feet
Plant patent:	4601

UNIQUE FEATURES

Flower:	Not showy
Fruit:	None
Foliage:	Outstanding rainbow of fall colors
Bark:	Similar to species
Growth rate:	Good (9 to 15 inches)
Root structure and depth:	Good
Pest and disease resistance:	No diseases or pests

Moraine is a registered trademark of The Siebenthaler Co.

Liquidambar styraciflua. (Photo courtesy The Siebenthaler Co.)

Storm resistance:	Excellent
Salt tolerance:	Unknown
Other comments:	Winter hardy to –30°F. This is the cadillac of the sweetgums. Dark green, leathery summer foliage.

AVAILABLE FROM

The Siebenthaler Company, Dayton, OH

Manbeck Nurseries, Inc., New Knoxville, OH

Decker Nurseries, Groveport, OH

Moller Nurseries, Inc., Gresham, OR

DESCRIPTION

Common name:	**Park Osage orange**
Botanical name:	*Maclura pomifera inermis* 'Park'
Parentage:	Selection
Hardiness zone:	4 to 8
Mature size:	50 feet, typical of species

UNIQUE FEATURES

Flower:	Male strain
Fruit:	None
Foliage:	Glossy deep green
Bark:	Exfoliating
Growth rate:	Medium

Site requirements:	Virtually any
Pest and disease resistance:	Yes
Storm resistance:	Yes
Other comments:	Extremely drought-tolerant and able to withstand cold winters

AVAILABLE FROM

Willis Nursery Co., Ottawa, KS

DESCRIPTION

Common name:	**Southern Magnolia**
Botanical name:	*Magnolia grandiflora*
Hardiness zone:	7
Mature size:	Height: 60 to 80 feet Spread: 30 to 50 feet

UNIQUE FEATURES

Flower:	Large, creamy white, frequent in May
Fruit:	Red, splits open to expose seeds, cucumber-shaped pods
Foliage:	Dark green, long and narrow, evergreen
Growth rate:	Slow, develops into large tree
Root structure and depth:	Deep and fibrous
Pest and disease resistance:	Excellent
Other comments:	Tolerates shade, needs room

AVAILABLE FROM

Wayside Gardens, Hodges, SC
Bobtown Nursery, Onanock, VA

DESCRIPTION

Common name:	**Galaxy Magnolia**
Botanical name:	*Magnolia stellata* 'Galaxy'
Parentage (if hybrid):	Developed at the U.S. National Arboretum
Hardiness zone:	5
Mature size:	Height: 40 to 50 feet Spread: 10 to 15 feet

UNIQUE FEATURES

Flower:	3-inch diameter, white, April before leaves, fragrant

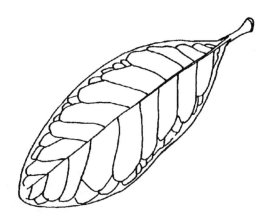

Fruit:	Seldom-produced pod
Foliage:	Dark green in summer, yellow-bronze in fall, thick when grown in full sun, large leaves
Bark:	Brown
Growth rate:	Slow
Root structure and depth:	Fleshy roots, needs deep soil
Pest and disease resistance:	Excellent
Storm resistance:	Good
Other comments:	Best grown with northern exposure in northern climate to protect blooms

AVAILABLE FROM

Lake County Nursery, Perry, OH

DESCRIPTION

Common name:	**Centurion Crabapple**
Botanical name:	*Malus* 'Centurion'
Hardiness zone:	4
Mature size:	Height: 26 feet Spread: 15 feet

Malus 'Centurion'. (*Photo courtesy Lake County Nursery.*)

Malus 'Centurion'.

UNIQUE FEATURES

Flower:	Single, rose-red
Fruit:	Cherry red, $\frac{5}{8}$-inch diameter, persistent
Foliage:	Dark green, reddish cast, glossy
Growth rate:	Good
Site requirements:	Sandy loam, moist, sun or part shade
Pest and disease resistance:	Tolerant of most diseases
Other comments:	Upright form, straight, well-branched tree

AVAILABLE FROM

Many nurseries

DESCRIPTION

Common name:	**Harvest Gold Crabapple**
Botanical name:	*Malus* 'Harvest Gold'
Hardiness zone:	4
Mature size:	Height: 20 feet Spread: 15 feet

UNIQUE FEATURES

Flower:	White, pink buds, single, abundant, later than other crabapples

Malus 'Harvest Gold'. (*Photo courtesy Lake County Nursery.*)

Malus 'Harvest Gold'.

Fruit:	Golden, $\frac{1}{2}$-inch diameter, persistent
Foliage:	Dark green
Growth rate:	Vigorous
Pest and disease resistance:	Extremely tolerant
Other comments:	Upright growth

AVAILABLE FROM

1. Appalachian Nurseries, Waynesboro, PA
2. Bailey Nurseries, Inc., St. Paul, MN
3. Carlton Plants, Dayton, OR
4. Femrite Nursery Company, Aurora, OR
5. Furr's Northwest Propagation, Sandy, OR
6. Leo Gentry Wholesale Nursery, Gresham, OR
7. C. M. Hobbs & Sons, Inc., Bridgeport, IN
8. John Holmlund Nursery Company, Gresham, OR
9. King Nursery, Montgomery, IL
10. Lincoln Nurseries, Inc., Grand Rapids, MI
11. A. McGill & Son, Fairview, OR
12. Moller's Nursery, Inc., Gresham, OR
13. Mount Arbor Nurseries, Shenandoah, IA
14. Nappe & Son Nursery, Boring, OR
15. Hans Nelson & Sons Nursery, Inc., Boring, OR
16. Pacific Coast Nursery, Inc., Grand Haven, MI
17. Raintree Farms, Franklin, IN
18. Ran-Pro Farms, Inc., Tayler, TX
19. Riverwood Growers, Oquawka, IL
20. Schichtel's, Orchard Park, NY
21. Simpson Nursery Company, Vincennes, IN
22. Speer & Sons Nursery, Inc., Hillsboro, OR
23. Surface Nursery, Inc., Gresham, OR
24. Kelly Nurseries of Dansville, Dansville, NY

DESCRIPTION

Common name:	**Sugar Tyme Crabapple**

Malus 'Sugar Tyme.' (*Photo courtesy Lake County Nursery.*)

Botanical name:	*Malus* 'Sugar Tyme'
Hardiness zone:	4
Mature size:	Height: 18 feet Spread: 15 feet
Plant patent:	Applied for

UNIQUE FEATURES

Flower:	White, pale pink buds, fragrant
Fruit:	Bright red, ½-inch diameter, persistent through autumn and winter
Foliage:	Green and clean
Growth rate:	Vigorous
Pest and disease resistance:	Excellent
Other comments:	Upright, oval, award winner

AVAILABLE FROM

Many nurseries

DESCRIPTION

Common name:	**Black Tupelo**
Botanical name:	*Nyssa sylvatica*
Parentage:	Native
Hardiness zone:	4
Mature size:	Height: 90 feet Spread: 35 to 40 feet

UNIQUE FEATURES

Flower:	Inconspicuous, sexes separate
Fruit:	Small blue berry
Foliage:	Dense, leathery, dark green, brilliant scarlet, orange in autumn
Root structure and depth:	Difficult to transplant, move small trees only
Site requirements:	Rich, moist loam, sun or partial shade, native to swamplands
Pest and disease resistance:	Excellent

Storm resistance:	Excellent
Salt resistance:	Excellent
Other comments:	Pyramidal growth habit

AVAILABLE FROM

Many nurseries

DESCRIPTION

Common name:	**Hop Hornbeam**
Botanical name:	*Ostrya virginiana*
Parentage:	Native to eastern half of United States
Hardiness zone:	3
Mature size:	Height: 60 feet Spread: 25 to 30 feet

UNIQUE FEATURES

Flower:	Catkins
Fruit:	Bladderlike pods, like hops
Foliage:	Dense, bright green, golden-yellow in autumn, persistent brown in winter
Bark:	Slender, spreading branches, finely shredded dark brown bark
Growth rate:	Slow

Root structure and depth:	Difficult to transplant, spring only, container or BB
Site requirements:	Medium loam, dry or moist, sun or shade, pH of 6.0 to 7.5
Pest and disease resistance:	Fairly free of disease, excellent pest resistance
Other comments:	Pyramidal; once established, becomes a handsome tree

AVAILABLE FROM

Many nurseries

DESCRIPTION

Common name:	**Sourwood**
Botanical name:	*Oxydendrum arboreum*
Parentage:	Native
Hardiness zone:	5
Mature size:	Height: 25 to 30 feet Spread: 10 to 15 feet

UNIQUE FEATURES

Flower:	Small white, racemes, late summer, lily-of-the-valley-like flowers
Fruit:	Dried capsules
Foliage:	Dense, leathery, glossy, dark green, brilliant scarlet in autumn

Growth rate:	Slow
Site requirements:	High-organic loam, moist, well-drained, sun or shade
Other comments:	Graceful pyramidal shape

AVAILABLE FROM

Many nurseries

DESCRIPTION

Common name:	**Persian Parrotia**
Botanical name:	*Parrotia persica*
Parentage:	Introduced in 1840
Hardiness zone:	5
Mature size:	Height: 20 to 40 feet Spread: 15 to 30 feet

UNIQUE FEATURES

Flower:	Crimson in March or April
Fruit:	Small brown capsule

Foliage:	Reddish purple in spring to medium green, to yellow, orange, and scarlet
Bark:	Exfoliating gray, green, white, and brown
Growth rate:	Medium
Site requirements:	Well-drained; tolerant, once established
Pest and disease resistance:	Excellent
Other comments:	Sometimes grows with several trunks

AVAILABLE FROM

Weston Nurseries, Hopkinton, MA

DESCRIPTION

Common name:	**Bloodgood London Plane Tree**
Botanical name:	*Plantanus acerifolia* 'Bloodgood'
Parentage (if hybrid):	American x Oriental
Hardiness zone:	5
Mature size:	Height: 100 feet Spread: 50 feet

UNIQUE FEATURES

Fruit:	Pendulous, ball-like clusters of seed

Plantanus acerifolia 'Bloodgood'.

Foliage:	Large, coarse, maple-leaf-shaped leaves, yellow-brown in autumn
Bark:	Conspicuous, exfoliating bark, light creamy inner bark color
Growth rate:	Rapid growth, tolerates heavy pruning
Site requirements:	Adapts to adverse soil, tolerates heat and drought
Pest and disease resistance:	Resistance to anthracnose
Salt tolerance:	Excellent
Other comments:	Very tolerant of city conditions

AVAILABLE FROM

Many local nurseries

DESCRIPTION

Common name:	**Sargent Cherry**

Botanical name:	*Prunus sargentii*
Parentage:	Introduced from Japan in 1890
Hardiness zone:	4
Mature size:	Height: 35 to 50 feet Spread: 25 to 40 feet

UNIQUE FEATURES

Flower:	Single, deep pink, $1\frac{1}{4}$-inch diameter, early spring, hardy bloom
Fruit:	Inconspicuous and black
Foliage:	Dense, bronze in spring, turning dark green in summer, orange-red in autumn
Bark:	Red cherry to dark brown
Growth rate:	Fast, 20-year life span
Site requirements:	Sandy loam to silty clay, moist, well-drained, sun
Pest and disease resistance:	Moderate
Salt tolerance:	Good
Other comments:	Most hardy ornamental cherry, transplant in spring only, upright shape, does not like smog

AVAILABLE FROM

Most nurseries

DESCRIPTION

Common name:	**Aristocrat Pear**
Botanical name:	*Pyrus calleryana* 'Aristocrat'
Parentage:	Probably a mutation seedling
Hardiness zone:	Generally accepted zones 5 through 9, but reports of hardiness in zone 4
Mature size:	Height: 30 to 35 feet, rarely as tall as 40 feet Spread: 25 to 30 feet
Plant patent:	3193, also trademarked in 1982

UNIQUE FEATURES

Flower:	Profuse white flowers before foliage
Fruit:	$\frac{1}{4}$- to $\frac{1}{2}$-inch diameter and persists until soft, when consumed by birds
Foliage:	Wavey, glossy, pointed, shimmers, red to orange in late autumn
Bark:	Chestnut to reddish brown, rough with age
Growth rate:	Rapid as a young tree, slows after 8 years
Root structure and depth:	Roots deep to moderately deep
Pest and disease resistance:	High resistance to fire blight and most foliar diseases. Resistant to most insects, and foliage remains clean.

Pyrus calleryana 'Aristocrat'. (*Photo courtesy Carlisle Nursery.*)

Storm resistance:	It has a national reputation for excellent storm resistance and resistance to wind damage.
Shape:	It has a central leader, strong branches with few sharp-angled crotches.
Other comments:	Holds up very well to city pollution. Acceptance has steadily increased nationally since Aristocrat was introduced in 1972, and sales have doubled for each of the last 4 years.

AVAILABLE FROM

Carlisle Nursery, Inc., Independence, KY
Carlisle has licensed about 75 nurseries in 22 states to propagate and distribute Aristocrat Pear and maintains a national list of firms that have Aristocrat Pear in landscape sizes.

DESCRIPTION

Common name:	**Redspire Pear**
Botanical name:	*Pyrus calleryana* 'Redspire'
Hardiness zone:	4
Mature size:	Height: 30 to 40 feet Spread: 20 to 30 feet
Plant patent:	3815

UNIQUE FEATURES

Flower:	White clusters of flowers, more flowers than Bradford
Fruit:	Same as Bradford, may even be less prominently occurring

Foliage:	Round leaves are thin, shiny, dark green and turn more yellow than red in fall. Colors ahead of Bradford.
Bark:	Brown, nondescriptive
Growth rate:	Medium-size tree
Root structure and depth:	Roots are relatively shallow and fibrous depending on soil conditions.
Pest and disease resistance:	More disease-resistant than Bradford.
Storm resistance:	Wider crotch in branches but more storm-resistant
Salt tolerance:	Will tolerate minimum amount of salt
Other comments:	A variety of improved Bradford

AVAILABLE FROM

Greenleaf Nursery, Park Hill, OK

DESCRIPTION

Common name:	**Red Oak**
Botanical name:	*Quercis rubra (borealis)*
Parentage:	Native
Hardiness zone:	3
Mature size:	Height: 75 feet

UNIQUE FEATURES

Flower:	Catkins, male and female
Fruit:	Round acorn 1 inch long
Foliage:	Dense, makes heavy shade, glossy green-red in autumn
Growth rate:	Vigorous
Root structure and depth:	Fibrous, transplants moderately

Site requirements:	Medium loam, moist, well-drained, sun
Pest and disease resistance:	Moderate
Storm resistance:	Excellent
Other comments:	Tolerant of urban conditions, clean habit; sweating procedure necessary when planting before leaf break

AVAILABLE FROM

Most nurseries

DESCRIPTION

Common name:	**Regent Scholartree**
Botanical name:	*Sophora japonica* 'Regent'
Parentage (if hybrid):	Selection of *S. japonica*
Hardiness zone:	4
Mature size:	Height: 50 to 70 feet Spread: 30 to 40 feet
Plant patent:	2338

UNIQUE FEATURES

Flower:	Showy, white, August, upright clusters, pea-shaped
Fruit:	Yellowish pods, persistent through winter
Foliage:	Glossy, dark green, compound, yellow in autumn

Bark:	Green bark and stems, smooth
Growth rate:	Fast, straight, large crown
Site requirements:	Sun, any soil
Pest and disease resistance:	Excellent
Salt tolerance:	Excellent
Other comments:	Tolerates heat and city conditions, vase shape

AVAILABLE FROM

Many nurseries

DESCRIPTION

Common name:	**Coral Fire Mountain Ash**
Botanical name:	*Sorbus hupehensis* 'Coral Fire'
Hardiness zone:	2 for northern hardiness and 8 for southern hardiness
Mature size:	Height: 20 to 25 feet Spread: 15 to 18 feet
Plant patent:	Registered trademark

UNIQUE FEATURES

Flower:	White, single blossom in spring
Fruit:	Coral-red, borne in late summer
Foliage:	Thick, green during the summer with brilliant red fall color
Bark:	Copper-colored during summer, reddish during fall
Growth rate:	Rapid
Root structure and depth:	Spreading, fibrous, depth to approximately 4 to 6 feet
Pest and disease resistance:	Resistant to fire blight
Storm resistance:	Good resistance to storm damage; not very brittle
Salt tolerance:	Fair
Other comments:	An excellent street tree for its flowers, foliage, and berries; but best noted for its uniform shape and growth habit. Can be easily trained into a lifted form with branching starting anywhere from 6 to 10 feet, depending on municipal requirements. Origin is in mountainous regions of Tibet.

AVAILABLE FROM

Pacific Coast Nursery, Inc., Portland, OR
Speer & Sons Nursery, Hillsboro, OR
Handy Nursery Company, Portland, OR
Zelenka Evergreen Nursery, Inc., Grand Haven, MI

DESCRIPTION

Common name:	**Ivory Silk Tree Lilac**
Botanical name:	*Syringa reticulata* 'Ivory Silk'
Parentage:	Selection by Sheridan Nursery
Hardiness zone:	3
Mature size:	Height: 25 to 35 feet Spread: 15 feet

UNIQUE FEATURES

Flower:	July bloom; large creamy, white clusters; begins at young age, poor-quality fragrance
Fruit:	Inconspicuous
Foliage:	Larger than common lilac, blue-green color
Bark:	Cherrylike, glossy
Growth rate:	Medium
Site requirements:	Sunny
Pest and disease resistance:	Susceptible to borers and scale, mildew
Other comments:	Sturdy, compact, oval growth habit, uniform shape

AVAILABLE FROM

Sheridan Nursery, Charles City, IA
Bailey Nursery, St. Paul, MN

Lake County Nursery, Perry, OH
Princeton Nursery, Princeton, NJ

DESCRIPTION

Common name:	**Sterling Silver Linden**
Botanical name:	*Tilia tomentosa* 'Sterling Silver'
Parentage:	Selection from species
Hardiness zone:	4
Mature size:	Height: 40 to 50 feet Spread: 25 to 30 feet
Plant patent:	Applied for

UNIQUE FEATURES

Flower:	Small, yellow, very fragrant
Fruit:	Warty nut
Foliage:	Green above, white and pubescent below
Growth rate:	Faster than other lindens
Pest and disease resistance:	Best of all lindens
Salt tolerance:	Excellent
Other comments:	Erect branches, susceptible to air pollution, tolerates heat and drought, broad pyramidal

AVAILABLE FROM

Most nurseries

DESCRIPTION

Common name:	**Chase tree**
Botanical name:	*Vitex agnus-castus*
Hardiness zone:	7
Mature size:	Height: 15 to 20 feet

UNIQUE FEATURES

Flower:	Continuously June to September, spectacular
Fruit:	Inconspicuous
Foliage:	Five leaflets, feathery gray
Bark:	Gray, blackish
Growth rate:	Fast

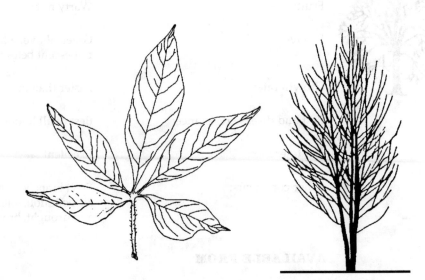

Pest and disease resistance: Excellent

Site requirements: Loves summer heat

AVAILABLE FROM

Weston Nurseries, Hopkinton, MA

DESCRIPTION

Common name: **Green Vase Zelkova**

Botanical name: *Zelkova serrata* 'Green Vase'

Parentage (if hybrid):   Seedling of *Z. serrata* 'Village Green'

Hardiness zone: 5

Mature size: Height: 60 to 70 feet
Spread: 50 to 60 feet

Plant patent: 5080

UNIQUE FEATURES

Flower and fruit: Not significant

Foliage: Narrow, serrate, bright green in summer and orange in fall

Bark: Exfoliating, attractive

Growth rate: Rapid, twice as fast as 'Village Green'

Root structure and depth: Deep

Pest and disease resistance: Excellent

Zelkova serrata 'Green Vase'. (*Photo courtesy J. Frank Schmidt Nursery.*)

Storm resistance:

Excellent

Salt tolerance:

Satisfactory and is tolerant of air pollution and heat

Other comments:

The Green Vase Zelkova has the vase-shaped branching habit of our native American Elm, but is not susceptible to Dutch Elm disease. It is taller than and not so broad as Village Green Zelkova when mature.

Green Vase Zelkova is the first shade tree to win the prestigious Styer Award of Garden Merit from the Pennsylvania Horticultural Society.

AVAILABLE FROM

Princeton Nursery, Princeton, NJ

J. Frank Schmidt Nurseries, Boring, OR

Pacific Coast Nurseries, Portland, OR

Commercial Nursery, Deckherd, TN
Plus many local nurseries and landscape contractors

Appendix B

Recommended Trees from Various Cities

Recommended Street Trees Being Planted in Selected Cities

Botanical name	Oak Park, IL	Huntsville, AL	Wellesley, MA	Modesto, CA	Vancouver, B.C.	Chicago, IL	Indianapolis, IN	Atlanta, GA
Acer buergerianum				*				
A. campestre	*		*				*	*
A. ginnala	*		*					
A. griseum			*					
A. nigrum			*					
A. palmatum varieties		*			*			
A. platanoides varieties			*			*	*	*
A. rubrum varieties			*			*	*	*
A. saccharum varieties			*			*	*	*
Aesculus hippocastanum 'Baumann'			*					
Alnus glutinosa pyramidalis	*		*					
Amelanchier canadensis 'Tradition' *grandiflora*			*					
Betula nigra 'Heritage'	*		*					*
B. platyphylia 'Whitespire'			*					
Carpinus betulas varieties	*	*	*		*		*	*
C. caroliniana	*		*			*		
Celtis occidentalis varieties	*			*		*	*	
Cercis canadensis	*							

Recommended Street Trees Being Planted in Selected Cities (Continued)

Botanical name	Oak Park, IL	Huntsville, AL	Wellesley, MA	Modesto, CA	Vancouver, B.C.	Chicago, IL	Indianapolis, IN	Atlanta, GA
Ceridiphyllum japonicum	*	*	*		*			
Chionanthus virginicus			*					
Cladrastis lutea		*	*		*			
Cornus kousa varieties		*	*		*			
C. mas		*			*			
C. nuttallii		*			*			
Corylus colurna		*			*	*	*	
Crataequs species	*	*	*		*		*	*
Eucommia ulmoides		*		*	*		*	
Fraxinus americana varieties		*	*	*	*	*	*	
F. excelsior varieties	*		*	*		*	*	*
F. pennsylvanica varieties			*	*			*	*
F. quadrangulata	*							
Ginkgo biloba—male varieties	*	*	*	*	*	*	*	
Gleditsia triacanthos inermis varieties	*	*	*	*	*	*	*	*
Gymnocladus dioicus	*		*			*		
Halesia carolina	*							
H. monticola		*			*			
Ilex opaca		*		*	*			
Koelreuteria paniculata		*	*	*	*			
Liquidambar styraciflua		*	*		*			*
Liriodendron tulipifera	*	*	*	*	*	*		
Maackia amurensis		*			*			
Maclura pomifera 'Park'			*					
Magnolia species	*	*		*	*			
Malus species	*	*	*		*		*	*
Nyssa sylvatica		*	*	*				
Ostrya virginiana	*	*	*		*			*
Oxydendron arboreum		*	*		*			
Parrotia persica		*			*			
Phellodendron amurense	*	*			*	*		
Pinus species				*				
Pistachia atlantica				*				
Plantanus acerifolia 'Bloodgood'	*	*	*	*	*		*	*

Recommended Street Trees Being Planted in Selected Cities (Continued)

Botanical name	Oak Park, IL	Huntsville, AL	Wellesley, MA	Modesto, CA	Vancouver, B.C.	Chicago, IL	Indianapolis, IN	Atlanta, GA
Prunus species			*					
Pseudotsuga menziesi			*					
Pyrus calleryana varieties	*	*	*	*	*	*	*	*
Quercus species	*	*	*	*	*	*	*	*
Sophora japonica 'Regent'	*	*	*		*		*	
Stewartia pseudo-camellia		*			*			
Styrax japonicum		*	*		*			
Syringa amurensis	*				*			
S. japonica	*	*						
Taxodium distichum		*			*			
Tilia americana						*		
T. cordata varieties			*	*		*	*	*
T. euchlora varieties	*	*			*	*	*	*
T. platphyllos	*							
T. tomentosa	*		*					*
Tsuga caroliniana			*					
Ulmus americana varieties			*			*		
U. parvifolia		*			*		*	
Zelkova serrata varieties	*	*	*		*	*	*	

The species and variety designations above refer to the best available trees, suited to the local urban environment of each city.
SOURCES: Master street tree plans from each of the cities listed.

Comparison of Various City Forestry Programs

Comparison of Municipal Forestry Departments

Items of comparison	Albion, MI	Anko, MN	Jamestown, ND	Swift Current, Saskatchewan	Wellesley, MA	Westerville, OH
Population	11,095	16,000	16,000	16,200	27,000	30,000
Inventory	Yes	No	Yes	No	Yes	Yes
Computerized	No	No	Yes	No	Yes	No
Tree count	5700	18,000	7327	—	12,760	5000
Master plan	Yes	Yes	No	No	Yes	Yes
Age of plan, years	4	8	—	—	1	2
Regulations	Yes	Yes	Yes	No	Yes	Yes
Planting regulations	Yes	Yes	Yes	No	Yes	Yes
Pruning regulations	Yes	Yes	Yes	No	Yes	Yes
Removal regulations	Yes	Yes	Yes	No	Yes	Yes
Routine pruning time	—	—	0%	75%	40%	15%
Emergency time	—	—	0%	10%	10%	4%
Electric time	—	—	5%	0%	45%	75%
Demand time	—	0%	0%	15%	5%	4%
Budget per tree	$10.40	$4.06	$7.32	—	$10.00	$27.00
Budget per capita	$5.14	$5.28	$3.35	$11.23 (Canadian dollars)	$5.04	$4.50
Removals (% of budget)	—	48%	28%	26%	9%	44%
Administration	—	41%	64%	6%	17%	4%
Trimming	—	11%	2%	40%	39%	44%
Planting	9%	—	6%	28%	22%	8%
Policy for replacements	$5000	—	—	Downtown	1 for 1	—
Tree City—USA	Yes	Yes	Yes	No	Yes	Yes
Champion search	No	Yes	No	—	Yes	No
Advisory board	Yes	Yes	Yes	No	Yes	Yes

Research programs	No	No	No	No	Yes	Yes
Research money	—	—	—	—	$0.10 per capita	—
Arborist on staff	Yes	No	Yes	No	Yes	Yes
Years on job	10	10	8	18	22	25
Organizations/ISA chapters	SMA, ISA, Mich.	Minn.	SMA, ISA, N.Dak.	SMA, ISA	SMA, ISA, Mass.	SMA
Certified arborist	No	Yes	No	No	Yes	No
Annual training	No	Yes	No	—	Yes	Yes
Trees per employee	—	9000	7327	—	2550	12,500
Training hours per employee per year	—	4	40	No	50	16
CPR training	—	Yes	Yes	No	Yes	Yes
Pesticides license	—	Yes	Yes	Yes	Yes	Yes
Employees with license	0	2	1	1	3	5
Pruning cycle, years	10	7	—	—	3	3 maximum

Comparison of Municipal Forestry Departments (Continued)

Items of comparison	Grand Forks, ND	Bismarck, ND	Cleveland Heights, OH	West Allis, WI	Ft. Collins, CO	Chicago, IL
Population	44,000	50,000	56,000	65,000	90,000	2,783,726
Inventory	Yes	Yes	Yes	Yes	Yes	Yes
Computerized	No	Yes	No	Yes	Yes	No
Tree count	23,500	15,000	50,000	18,900	20,000	440,943
Master plan	No	Yes	Yes	Yes	Yes	Yes
Age of plan, years	—	10	33	?	2	1
Regulations	Yes	Yes	Yes	Yes	Yes	Yes
Planting regulations	No	Yes	No	Yes	Yes	Yes
Pruning regulations	No	Yes	Yes	No	Yes	Yes
Removal regulations	No	Yes	Yes	Yes	Yes	Yes
Routine pruning time	78%	85%	10%	80%	65%	32%
Emergency time	2%	15%	5%	10%	5%	2%
Electric time	0%	0%	1%	0%	0%	0%
Demand time	20%	0%	85%	10%	30%	0%
Budget per tree	$22.06	$13.40	$5.40	$22.06	$17.50	$28.18
Budget per capita	$6.41	$4.02	$4.82	$6.41	$3.89	$4.59
Removals (% of budget)	20%	—	30%	13%	40%	26%
Administration	25%	—	30%	20%	20%	5%
Trimming	30%	—	30%	45%	20%	40%
Planting	25%	—	10%	22%	20%	8%
Policy for replacements	1 for 1	By permit	Request	All sites	3 plantings per removal	Major program citywide
Tree City—USA	Yes	Yes	Yes	Yes	Yes	Yes
Champion search	Yes	Yes	No	No	No	Yes
Advisory board	Yes	Yes	No	Yes	No	Yes
Research programs	Yes	Yes	No	No	Yes	Yes

Research money	$4000	$600	—	—	—	—
Arborist on staff	Yes	No	Yes	Yes	Yes	Yes
Years on job	15	22	10	15	11	20
Organizations/ISA chapters	SMA, ISA	SMA, ISA, N.Dak.	SMA, ISA	SMA, ISA, Wis.	SMA, ISA	SAF, SMA, ISA
Certified arborist	No	No	No	Yes	No	Yes
Annual training	Yes	Yes	Yes	Yes	Conferences	Yes
Trees per employee	3917	2500	10,000	1050	2860	2598
Training hours per employee per year	16	180	30	160	No	16
CPR training	No	Yes	No	Yes	No	Yes
Pesticides license	Yes	Yes	Yes	Yes	No	Yes
Employees with license	4	1	0	3	0	4
Pruning cycle, years	6	—	10	7–9	8	6

Comparison of Municipal Forestry Departments (Continued)

Items of comparison	Ann Arbor, MI	Lansing, MI	Modesto, CA	Huntsville, AL	Wichita, KS	Toledo, OH
Population	107,000	130,000	150,000	164,000	280,000	380,000
Inventory	Yes	Yes	Yes	Partial	Yes	Yes
Computerized	Yes	No	Yes	No	No	Yes
Tree count	38,000	40,000	85,000	22,300	76,000	104,000
Master plan	No	No	Yes	Yes	No	No
Age of plan, years	—	—	3	2	—	—
Regulations	Yes	Yes	Yes	Yes	Yes	Yes
Planting regulations	Yes	Yes	Yes	Yes	Yes	Yes
Pruning regulations	Yes	Yes	Yes	Yes	Yes	Yes
Removal regulations	Yes	Yes	Yes	Yes	Yes	Yes
Routine pruning time	25%	86%	75%	Very little	23%	50%
Emergency time	5%	4%	1%	High	11%	25%
Electric time	0%	0%	0%	None	22% (removals)	0%
Demand time	70%	10%	24%	Very high	44%	0%
Budget per tree	$22.36	$16.25	$17.65	$6.99	$15.53	$14.27
Budget per capita	$7.94	$5.00	$10.00	$0.95	$4.21	$3.91
Removals (% of budget)	—	10%	10%	—	41%	26%
Administration	—	30%	13%	—	10%	20%
Trimming	—	42%	53%	—	41%	51%
Planting	—	18%	24%	—	8%	1%
Policy for replacements	Any location	Residential first, then commercial	1 per lot and 5 for 1	Resident donations	Private or public	Private and public
Tree City—USA	Yes	Yes	Yes	No	Yes	Yes
Champion search	Yes	Yes	—	No	No	No
Advisory board	Yes	Yes	Yes	—	Yes	No
Research programs	Yes	Yes	—	—	No	Yes

Research money	$2000	$0.01 per capita	—	—	—	—
Arborist on staff	Yes	Yes	Yes	Yes	No	No
Years on job	14	21	10	6	24	2
Organizations/ISA chapters	SMA, ISA, Mich.	SMA, ISA, Mich.	ISA	—	SMA, ISA, Kan.	—
Certified arborist	No	No	Yes	—	No	Yes
Annual training	Yes	Yes	—	—	No	Yes
Trees per employee	2923	2667	2125	11,150	2533	4727
Training hours per employee per year	20	—	Yes	—	1 per year	Yes
CPR training	—	No	Yes	—	Yes	Yes
Pesticides license	Yes	Yes	Yes	—	No	Yes
Employees with license	1	2	4	—	—	2
Pruning cycle, years	9	16	3	—	12	7

Comparison of Municipal Forestry Departments (Continued)

Items of comparison	Cleveland, OH	San Jose, CA	Edmonton, Alberta
Population	520,000	730,000	785,465
Inventory	Yes	Yes	Yes
Computerized	Yes	Yes	No
Tree count	70,000	250,000	85,000
Master plan	No	Yes	No
Age of plan, years	—	5	—
Regulations	Yes	Yes	Yes
Planting regulations	Yes	Yes	Yes
Pruning regulations	Yes	Yes	Yes
Removal regulations	Yes	Yes	Yes
Routine pruning time	85%	80%	70%
Emergency time	10%	10%	20%
Electric time	0%	0%	0%
Demand time	5%	10%	10%
Budget per tree	$21.43	$5.60	$8.25 (Canadian dollars)
Budget per capita	$2.88	$1.92	$1.12 (Canadian dollars)
Removals (% of budget)	13%	4%	2%
Administration	13%	10%	18%
Trimming	67%	75%	50%
Planting	7%	11%	30%
Policy for replacements	—	New subdivision	1 for 1
Tree City—USA	Yes	Yes	No
Champion search	Yes	No	Yes
Advisory board	No	No	No
Research programs	No	Yes	Yes
Research money	—	$0.01 per capita	$1000 (Canadian dollars)
Arborist on staff	Yes	Yes	Yes
Years on job	10	21	22
Organizations/ISA chapters	SMA, ISA	SMA, ISA, Calif.	ISA, SMA
Certified arborist	No	No	—
Annual training	No	No	Yes
Trees per employee	2917	6757	4250
Training hours per employee per year	24	40	Yes
CPR training	Yes	No	—

Comparison of Municipal Forestry Departments (Continued)

Items of comparison	Cleveland, OH	San Jose, CA	Edmonton, Alberta
Pesticides license	Yes	Yes	Yes
Employees with license	2	7	2
Pruning cycle, years	7–10	8–10	5

Index

About the Author

Leonard E. Phillips, Jr. is a registered professional landscape architect in practice since 1963. Currently the Superintendent of the Park and Tree Division for the Town of Wellesley, Massachusetts, he is responsible for the landscape maintenance of all public open spaces, with an annual budget of more than $1 million. Mr. Phillips is a graduate of the University of Illinois, with degrees in both landscape architecture and ornamental horticulture. He has authored numerous articles and several books on landscaping and serves as editor of *City Trees*, the monthly journal of the Society of Municipal Arborists.